SIMPLY SEAFOOD

Seafood Cookery Made Easy

Basics for selection and preparation
of seafood from the Gulf of Mexico
to the Atlantic Provinces. With recipes
for saltwater and freshwater fish
and shellfish.

by Vicki Emmons

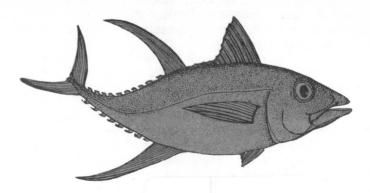

©
DeLorm
Free
ISBN 0-89933-043-6

Third Printing

D1111777

Dedication

To Richard, Elizabeth and Christina, with much love
and
to the memory of Pat and Ted Emmons of Islesford
whose love for Maine brought us here, to share its treasures.

◆ ◆

Acknowledgements

I offer my gratitude to the many people and organizations who have given valuable assistance and information in the preparation of this book.

To my family and friends, who offered their contributions to this book.

To Barbara Feller-Roth, my editor, who gave new meaning to the word "style." I would have been lost without her and her enthusiasm.

To Margaret Campbell, whose illustrations and design changed a book into a work of art.

To Susan Siens, whose typesetting labor gave form and character to my words.

To Bob Morrill, National Marine Fisheries Service, Portland, Maine; Mike Allsup, National Marine Fisheries Service, Gloucester, Mass.; John Jorgenson, Stinson Canning, Bath, Maine; Maine Department of Marine Resources; Joe Litchfield, Portland, Maine; Sea Grant Program, University of Maine, Orono; New Bedford Seafood Council, Fairhaven, Mass.; The Fishermen's Wives of Gloucester, Mass.; Massachusetts Seafood Council; Virginia Seafood Council; Mississippi Cooperative Extension Service; Texas Agricultural Extension Service, Texas A&M University; Sea Grant Marine Advisory Program, University of California Cooperative Extension; Bureau of Marketing and Extension Services, Florida Department of Natural Resources; National Fishery Educational Center, Chicago, Ill.; The Fishwife, Falmouth, Maine.

Table of Contents

Foreword   5
Preface   7

General Information

Buying Fish   10
Storing Fish   14
Cooking Methods   19

Saltwater Fish

Atlantic Croaker   34
Bluefish   36
Cod   40
Cusk   43
Eel   44
Haddock   48
Hake   53
Halibut   55
Herring   60
Mackerel   65
Ocean Perch   69
Pollock   73
Red Snapper   74
Salmon   76
Sea Bass   82
Shad   85
Shark   88
Smelt   91
Sole   94
Squid   101
Striped Bass   106
Swordfish   110
Tilefish   113
Tuna   116
Weakfish   123
Whiting   125

Freshwater Fish

Catfish   128
Frogs' Legs   130
Perch   132
Pike   135
Trout   138
Whitefish   141

Shellfish

Clams   146
Crab   152
Lobster   159
Mussels   167
Oysters   172
Periwinkles   177
Scallops   179
Shrimp   184

Chowders, Soups and Stews

193

Sauces & Marinades

207

Index

221

John's Foreword

When I made my living as a fisherman — some 30 years ago along the open ocean beaches of eastern Long Island and on the bays that embrace that windswept reach of land — I made many discoveries, among them how delicate, how sweet, how delightful a fresh fish properly cooked can be. I also began to understand what my fellow fishermen always told me. Asked if this fish, or that crab, or this oyster would be good to eat, they would invariably respond, ''There's nothing that lives in the sea that ain't good to eat.''

Eels, shad, shark, flounder and squid...and the more popular swordfish, weakfish, bluefish, striped bass and salmon...everything wrapped in scales or skin became my adventure. I prepared, cooked and tasted everything from the smallest minnows to whale steaks. And I dug, raked and hunted every kind of shellfish: hard clams, soft clams, skimmers and scallops.

I wish I'd read this book before I began my adventures with a fillet knife, or at the broiling pan. I could have learned more, and learned it faster. Because it's all here. The practical information, delivered in a practical and understandable way, the touches of culinary style that make a meal an experience, and the fish, in their true identity, drawn with accurate grace by Margaret Campbell and described in clean prose by Vicki Emmons.

I had to spend seven years fishing from dawn to dusk to learn what's in this book. You have only to keep it and read it to make a purely enjoyable discovery.

John N. Cole

Preface

Not until I lived along the coast did I discover how many varieties there are of fish and shellfish. It was surprising to me, however, that many of these were not readily available outside large cities. So much seafood goes from boat to truck to out of state, it's no wonder that many local cooks, faced with a limited selection, lose enthusiasm for fish cookery.

Presented here, therefore, are some unusual, interesting ways to prepare the usual selection of seafood. Recipes for several less familiar fish and shellfish are also included, with the hope that you will try something new. My wish is to create a renewed enthusiasm for fish cookery and to show that fish never needs to be ordinary. For a very reasonable price, you can offer your family a delicious, healthy and not-so-usual meal.

Bring fish and shellfish back to the table and let your enthusiasm catch on. You won't be sorry and my reason for writing this book will not have been in vain.

Vicki Emmons

General Information

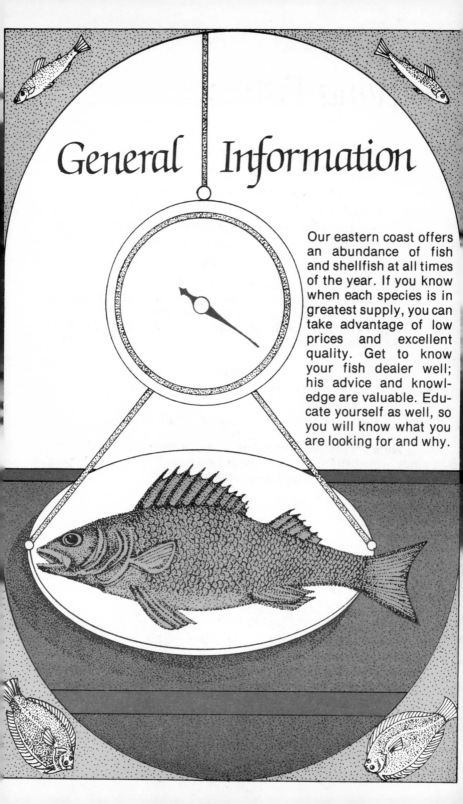

Our eastern coast offers an abundance of fish and shellfish at all times of the year. If you know when each species is in greatest supply, you can take advantage of low prices and excellent quality. Get to know your fish dealer well; his advice and knowledge are valuable. Educate yourself as well, so you will know what you are looking for and why.

Buying Fish

When you buy **whole fresh fish,** look for the following:

	fresh	old
skin	shiny, color unfaded	colorless, slimy
eyes	bright, clear, full	cloudy, pink
gills	red, free of slime	faded from pink to grey/brown
flesh	firm, elastic	skin separated from bones
odor	fresh, mild	strong, fishy

Note: Whole fish should not have bruises in the usable part of the flesh, which have been left by a pitchfork during unloading; the bruises can accelerate spoilage.

When you buy **cut fresh fish** (fillets, steaks or chunks), look for the following:

	fresh	old
flesh	firm, elastic, fresh-cut appearance	brown and/or dry edges
odor	fresh, mild	strong, fishy

Note: Fresh fish should be in moisture/vaporproof wrapping, with little or no air space between fish and wrapping material and little or no liquid in package.

ROUND FISH

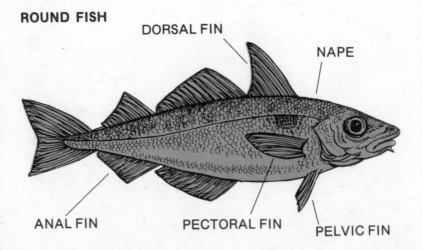

DORSAL FIN

NAPE

ANAL FIN

PECTORAL FIN

PELVIC FIN

Also, fish fillets displayed on a slant will lose juices and dry out.

When you buy **frozen fish,** be discriminating; check it carefully for the following:

	properly stored	**improperly stored**
flesh	solidly frozen, no pieces frozen together	discolored, freezer burn (drying) on surface
odor	not evident or very slight	strong, fishy
breaded products	clean, uniform appearance; breading/coating intact	
storage location	below ''load-line'' or ''frost-line'' of display freezer	

Note: Properly frozen fish should be in moisture/vapor-proof wrapping, which is close fitting and undamaged.

FLAT FISH

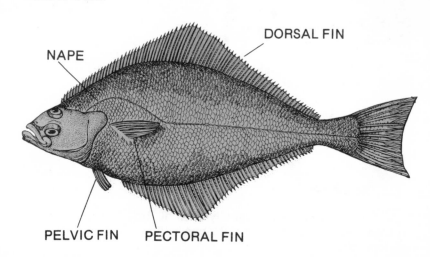

DORSAL FIN

NAPE

PELVIC FIN   PECTORAL FIN

Market Forms

Whole or Round Fish Sold as it comes from the water. Before cooking, it must be gutted, and gills and scales removed.

Drawn Fish One which has been gutted, with gills and scales removed.

Whole-Dressed Fish One which has had head, tail and fins removed, as well as having been scaled and gutted.

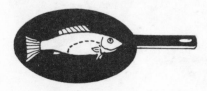

Pan-Dressed Fish Usually a small fish which has been scaled and gutted, but fits into pan without having head and tail removed.

Steaks Cross-section slices from a large, dressed fish.

Fillets Lengthwise cuts from the sides of a fish, cut away from the backbone; practically boneless, with skin on or off.

Butterfly Fillets The two sides/fillets joined along the back; good for grilling.

Sticks or Portions Pieces of fish cut from blocks of frozen fillets, uniform in size and weighing several ounces. Fish is sometimes coated with breading or batter and packaged raw, or cooked before freezing.

How Much To Buy

Market Form	Per Person	6 People
Whole	1 pound	5-6 pounds
Whole-dressed	1/2 pound	3 pounds
Fillets	1/3 - 1/2 pound	2-3 pounds
Steaks and chunks	1/3 - 1/2 pound	2-3 pounds

Storing Fish

Fresh fish Keep fresh fish in moistureproof wrapping, and pack in ice or keep refrigerated below 40°F at all times. Use within 2 days or freeze.

Frozen fish Store frozen fish in a freezer at 0°F. If stored at 10°F or above, hold no more than 1 week. Place in refrigerator to thaw, but do not store thawed fish longer than 24 hours or refreeze it, since it loses quality.

Shellfish See individual headings (clams, oysters, etc.).

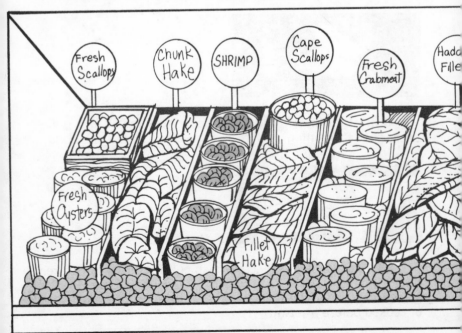

Freezing Fish

Rinse all fish before freezing, then follow one of the freezing methods most suitable for your type fish or seafood. Keep in mind that it is easier to defrost steaks and fillets that have been wrapped separately, or have been separated by layers of waxed paper inside their heavy outer wrap. This method facilitates easy separation and thawing for cooking.

PROTECTIVE DIPS

A good way to guard against oxidation and freezer burn is to dip the fish in any one of the following solutions before freezing. This method is useful for quantity freezing of bought or caught fish.

Lemon Juice-Gelatin Glaze. Place 1/4 cup of lemon juice in a 1-pint container and fill it to the top with water. Dissolve 1 packet of unflavored gelatin in 1/2 cup of the lemon juice/water mixture. Heat the remaining liquid to boiling, then stir the gelatin mixture into the hot liquid until it is well mixed. Cool the glaze to room temperature, then dip the cleaned fish into the glaze and drain it for a few seconds. Wrap the fish in clear

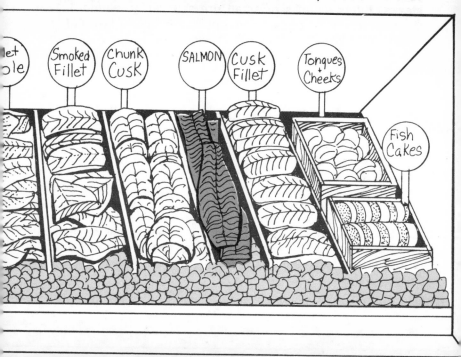

plastic wrap, smoothing out any air bubbles, then in heavier outer wrap. Label, date and place it in the coldest part of the freezer (0° to —16°F). With this method, storage times generally are 6 months for lean fish and 3 months for fatty fish.

Chilled 5% Brine. Dipping the fish into a solution of 2/3 cup of salt to 1 gallon of water prevents browning and reduces dripping during thawing and cooking lean fish, such as cod, flounder, haddock, etc. Immerse the cleaned fish for 30 seconds, then wrap it twice as for glazed fish and freeze. With this method, the storage life is up to 9 months.

Chilled 2 1/2% Brine. Freezing fish in a solution of 1/3 cup of salt to 1 gallon of water is good for oily fish, such as salmon, mackerel, bluefish, swordfish, and mullet. When the fish are frozen into ice blocks using a milk carton or other airtight container, the storage life is up to 6 months.

To freeze fish in plastic or glass containers with airtight covers made especially for the freezer, carefully pack the steaks, fillets, chunks or small dressed fish to within 1 1/2 inches of the top of a quart-size container or within 1 inch of the top of a pint-size container. Fill it with 2 1/2% brine until the fish is covered. Remove any air bubbles, seal tightly and freeze.

To freeze fish in milk cartons, cut off the lid-end, place the fish inside, cover with 2 1/2% brine and freeze. When frozen solid, reseal the open end tightly with aluminum foil.

Ice Glaze. Wrap the cleaned fish loosely with moisture-proof wrap and place the fish on a cookie sheet. Freeze it quickly at —20°F. When the fish is frozen solid, remove the wrap and dip the fish quickly in and out of ice-cold water. A thin coat of ice should form; if not, return the fish to the freezer a little while longer. Repeat dipping several times to thicken the ice, then carefully wrap the fish for the freezer. Label and store.

Thawing Fish

Refrigerator thawing is recommended whenever possible. Allow 18 to 24 hours for a 1-pound package. Since time is usually of the essence, however, I find that thawing in an airtight wrap in cold water works well and takes from 1 to 2 hours for a 1-pound package. Fish can be cooked frozen in most recipes, the exceptions being baked whole fish or pieces to be crumbed or battered before cooking. Frozen fillets and steaks can be baked, broiled or poached; just allow twice the cooking time.

When thawing solid ice block fish, hold it under cold water until the ice melts. Place the fish into an airtight wrap or bag; then place it in the refrigerator or in cold water to thaw.

For methods of freezing and thawing shellfish, see individual headings.

Packing Fish For Travel

You can safely transport almost all fish over long distances if you take the proper precautions.

Preparation Tips Handle the fish as little as possible. Dress or fillet the fish so it will be ready for the home freezer. Dress large fish, such as tuna, cod and amberjack; pack the body cavity with ice; then cover the entire fish with ice.

Superchilling Line the bottom of an insulated, lidded ice chest with 3 to 4 inches of flaked or crushed ice, over a rack if possible, to keep the fish out of the melting ice water. Layer the fish in a mixture of rock or table salt and crushed ice, using 1/2 pound of salt for 5 pounds of ice. Whole fish should be layered, unwrapped, in the ice. When the cooler is filled, top the fish with a generous layer of ice, close the lid tightly and secure the drain plug, if there is one. Place the chest in the coolest part of the car, **not** the trunk. If you are traveling for several days, drain off the melting water each night and add more ice and salt. Do not remove the fish from the cooler until you reach your final destination. At home, unpack and rinse the fish in fresh, cold water. Use it fresh the same day or freeze it using a glaze or brine. If there is any question of spoilage, don't take a chance; throw the fish away.

Nutritional Value ═══

Because of growing concern with good health and nutrition, there has been a rekindled interest in fish and shellfish as valuable sources of high-quality, low-calorie protein. Examples of those especially high in protein are tuna, halibut, cod, crab, scallops and lobster. Those with slightly lower protein content are trout, herring, oysters and clams.

Fish and shellfish are also easily digested, contain large amounts of essential vitamins and minerals, are low in sodium and contain mainly polyunsaturated fats.

SALTWATER FISH AND SHELLFISH

Lean

Clams	Fluke	Periwinkles	Shrimp
Cod	Haddock	Pollock	Sole
Crab	Halibut	Red Snapper	Squid
Croaker	Lobster	Scallops	Tilefish
Cusk	Mussels	Sea Bass	Whiting
Flounder	Oysters	Shark	

Moderately Fatty

Hake
Smelt
Striped Bass
Swordfish
Tuna

Fatty

Bluefish	Herring	Salmon	Shad
Eel	Mackerel	Sardines	Weakfish (Seatrout)

FRESHWATER FISH

Lean

Bass	Frogs' Legs	Pickerel	Walleye (Perch)
Burbot	Perch	Pike	

Fatty

Catfish
Lake Herring
Trout
Whitefish

Cooking Methods ═══

Since fish is naturally tender and delicate, it needs minimal cooking. Yet it continues to suffer cruel treatment in the kitchen, primarily due to overcooking. Small wonder that many of our memories of fish are less than pleasant!

This chapter is designed to supply you with sufficient basic cooking information to approach fish cookery with confidence.

━━━━━━━━▶━◆━◀━━━━━━━

Baking This method works best with whole fish, thick cuts of fish and fatty fish. Lean fish works well as long as it is basted often. Oven temperatures range from moderate (350°-375°F) to very hot (450°-500°F) and cooking times vary according to temperature. For example, if you are using a cooking temperature of 450°F, measure the fish at the thickest part and allow 10 minutes per inch of thickness. If the fish is frozen, cook twice the specified time or until the fish flakes easily when tested with a knife point at the thickest part, close to the bones in whole fish. When testing cuts of fish, the flesh should easily flake and have lost its translucent appearance, yet still be moist.

Hot Oven Baking, Spencer Method This is an easy way for fillets or steaks to be cooked quickly with a small amount of cooking fat. Preheat the oven to 500°-550°F. Cut 2 pounds of fish into 6 equal pieces. Dip the pieces first into salted milk (1 teaspoon of salt to 1 cup of milk) and then into **bread** crumbs (other crumbs won't work). Place the pieces in a well-greased baking dish and drizzle over them a small amount of melted butter. Place the baking dish in the upper part of the oven for about 10 minutes. Test the fish with a knife point for doneness. (A fork causes more damage to the fish.) Don't be tempted to add liquid; the fish will not burn. Serve with your favorite tartar sauce or make the one on page 216.

Broiling This method works best for the fatty fishes, although lean fish can be used if it is basted often. Steaks, fillets or split fish from 3/4 to 1 inch thick at the thickest part should be used; larger cuts will dry out before the fish is cooked through.

Broil the fish 3 to 4 inches from the heat in a preheated broiler, allowing 9 to 10 minutes per inch of thickness. If you are broiling frozen fish, place it farther from the heat and broil it 20 minutes per inch. To keep the fish moist during broiling, add water to the bottom of your broiling pan.

When you are broiling thin steaks (less than 1/2 inch thick), do not turn them or they will break apart. Baste them generously during cooking with any fat or oil in combination with lemon or lime juice, herbs and seasonings to create whatever flavor you wish.

To keep your kitchen smelling pleasant, simmer a cinnamon stick in 1 cup of water in a small saucepan while the fish is cooking.

Sauteing This method of cooking is best for thin, tender pieces of fish that can be cooked quickly over moderate to high heat. A combination of butter and oil prevents the fish from burning before it is fully cooked. Only a thin coating of flour should be used, if any coating is desired. The coating should be allowed to dry thoroughly before cooking; seasonings should be added after the fish is cooked. Take care not to crowd the fish into the skillet, and do not cover the pan, since the resulting steam will prevent the fish from becoming crisp.

Pan Frying Pan frying is one of the best ways to cook very small, whole fish, such as perch, smelt and trout. The fish can be dusted with seasoned cornmeal or flour and cooked in melted butter over low heat until the fish has browned on both sides and is thoroughly·cooked. Batters should not be used for pan frying, since the low heat causes the coating to become soggy.

As in sauteing, do not crowd the fish or use a cover, since steam will prevent the fish from becoming crisp. Large fish (longer than 8 inches) may burn if they are cooked in butter until they are done. A better method is to cook them first in hot oil until the fish begins to brown, then drain the oil from the pan and finish cooking the fish in butter.

I have found that nonstick skillets are a valuable aid in sauteing/pan frying. Fish, with or without a coating, tends to stick, especially when cooking in oil, and the results can be frustrating.

Deep Frying Lean fish and shellfish are best suited to this cooking method. For successful results, there are several important points worth noting.

1. Whatever oil or shortening you choose should be able to withstand temperatures up to 500°F without smoking or burning. Corn and peanut oils are recommended by some cooks; solid shortening is preferred by others. Experiment to find out which oils give you the best results.

2. Always use a thermometer, even if your deep fryer has a built-in thermostat. It is very important to maintain the oil temperature called for during cooking, and to return the oil to the proper cooking temperature before adding a new batch of fish.

3. Use uniform-size pieces of fish. Cook thin cuts (3/8 inch thick or less) for 1 to 2 minutes at 375°-380°F; cook thick cuts (more than 1 1/2 inches thick) for 4 to 5 minutes at 360°F.

4. Choosing a batter or coating will depend on the size of the fish pieces as well as personal preference. Thick batters work best on pieces of fish 1½ in. thick or more; thin batters are best for cuts 3/8 in. thick or less. For best results, both the fish and the batter should be ice-cold, unless the recipe states otherwise. This will prevent the coating from absorbing excess oil during cooking. When coating the fish with crumbs or any other dry coating, first dip the fish pieces into a beaten egg, then into the dry coating. Allow the pieces to dry on a cookie sheet in the refrigerator for at least 15 minutes. This chilling will prevent the fish and coating from absorbing excess oil during cooking.

5. Don't crowd the fish pieces in the pan, and allow enough oil to cover the fish while cooking. Always drain the cooked fish on paper towels, and serve the fish as soon as possible to retain crispness and flavor.

COOKING METHODS, continued

Poaching Poaching can be a successful cooking method for whole fish or smaller cuts, such as steaks and fillets. For best results, use firm-textured fish. Soft-fleshed fish falls apart during cooking. To cook, simmer the fish in enough seasoned broth (see page 205) to completely cover it. Poached fish is delicious served hot with a variety of sauces, from a simple seasoned butter sauce to a rich hollandaise sauce, or served chilled with a cold mayonnaise-based sauce.

When poaching a whole fish, the fish should fit the pan. It is a good idea to measure your poacher or pot before buying a whole fish, especially if you plan to serve the fish with head and tail intact. A good substitute for a poaching pan is a roasting pan with a cover, as long as it can heat evenly on top of your stove.

Always wrap a whole fish in several layers of cheesecloth to facilitate handling, before and after cooking. Leave several inches of cloth at the head and tail ends to knot and use as handles. The cloth will prevent the fish from breaking apart after cooking when you lift it from the pan. Take care to support a large fish in the middle when lifting it from the pan; otherwise, its weight will cause it to break in half. Transfer the fish to a serving platter and remove the cheesecloth from the fish when it is cool enough to handle. The skin can then be scraped carefully away with a sharp knife.

When poaching cuts of fish such as steaks or fillets, it is not necessary to use cheesecloth. It is helpful to place a rack in the bottom of the pan, however, to support the fish during cooking, and to allow for easier removal from the pan when the fish is cooked. The skin on fish steaks can easily be removed after cooking, but it is advisable to remove the skin from fillets prior to cooking.

There are several poaching methods and broths to choose from. Select the poaching broth that best suits your type of fish. The more herbs and seasonings you use, the longer you should simmer the broth before adding the fish. A court bouillon, for example, should simmer at least 20 minutes to develop the flavors. Some cooks lower the fish directly into the simmering liquid; others prefer to remove the pan from the heat, add the fish, then return the pan to the heat and bring the liquid to boiling. Once the liquid returns to a boil, lower the heat to a simmer, cover and begin timing; allow 9 to 10 minutes cooking time for every inch of thickness at the thickest part of the fish, or 6 to 8 minutes per pound. The fish should flake easily when it is cooked; a whole fish is best tested at the thickest point near the backbone to avoid blemishing the flesh.

Always reserve the poaching broth. It can be strained and frozen, to be used later in soups, chowders or sauces, or to poach another fish.

Grilling The best fish for grilling is a moderately fat to fat, firm-fleshed and full-flavored fish, such as salmon, trout, tuna, bluefish and swordfish. Almost any fish or shellfish can be successfully grilled, however, if it is properly handled.

Small cuts of fish cook best in hinged wire broilers; thick cuts can be cooked directly on well-greased grills. Cuts from 1 to 2 inches thick are best for grilling. They should be grilled slowly over medium to low heat so the fish will not overcook on the outside before it is done on the inside. Test frequently with a knife point for doneness.

To prevent drying, baste all cuts of fish frequently. Butter mixed with vegetable oil and lemon / lime juice works well. For additional flavoring, marinate the fish to firm up the flesh and allow for easier handling. (See Sauces and Marinades, page 207). Adding damp wood chips, especially hickory or maple, to the fire adds a wonderful, smoky flavor to the fish.

Remember to clean and oil your grill racks before using.

————— ▶·●·◀ —————

Basic Preparation ▬

How to dress a round fish:

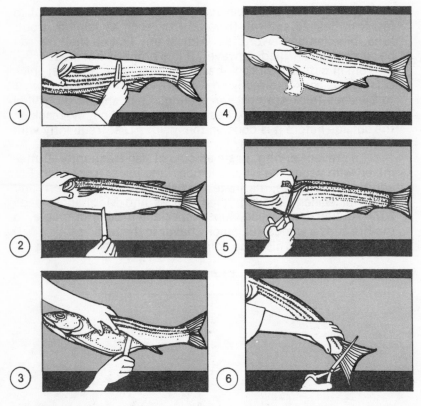

1   Scale fish.
2   and 3   Make slit in belly from head to anal fin.
4   Remove entrails.
5   and 6   Remove fins and tail fin. See also labeled diagram on page 10.

How to stuff a round fish:

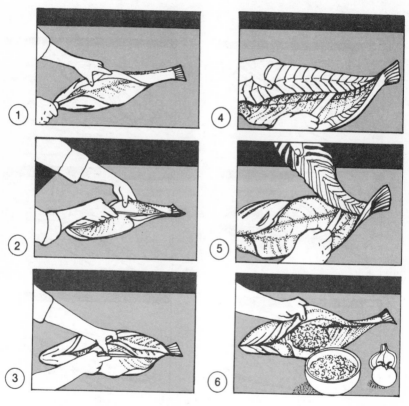

1 Cut towards head to enlarge cavity.
2 Starting at tail, cut flesh away from backbone and ribs.
3 Turn fish over and repeat step 2.
4 Free backbone from fish.
5 Cut backbone away at both ends.
6 Stuff cavity and secure opening with skewers or toothpicks.

How to fillet a round fish:

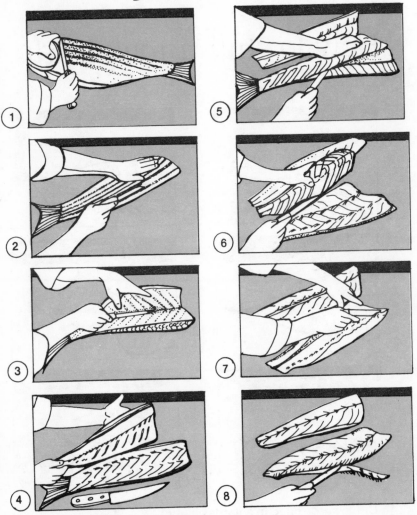

1 Cut head off behind gills.
2 Make lengthwise cut along back to tail.
3 and **4** Carefully cut flesh away from topside of backbone and ribs.
5 and **6** Slide knife under backbone and cut away as in steps 3 and 4.
7 and **8** Cut away fins and bony parts.

How to steak a round fish:

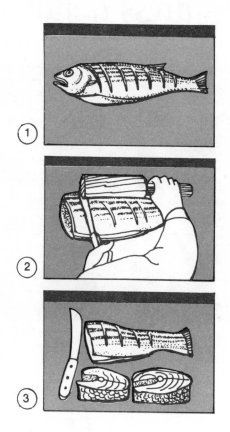

1 Mark steaks by cutting just to backbone.
2 Push knife through backbone with heavy utensil.
3 Finish cutting through other side to separate steak completely.

How to dress a flat fish:

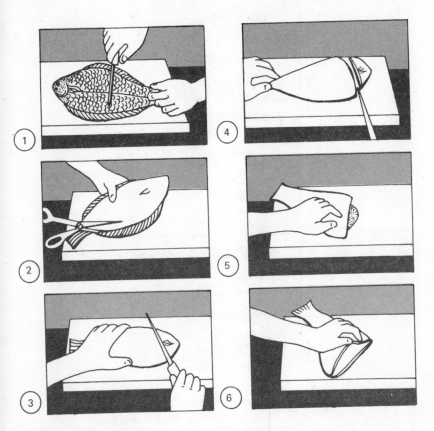

1 Remove scales.
2 Cut away fins.
3 and 4 Cut off head just behind pectoral fin.
5 Press body gently to push out entrails.
6 Clean out cavity.

How to stuff a flatfish:

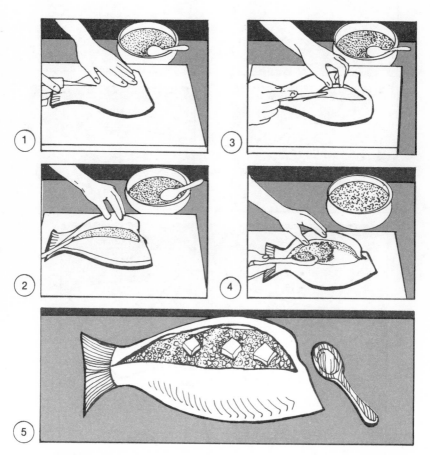

1. Make cut down center of underside of fish just to backbone.
2. and **3** Slide knife carefully along backbone to loosen flesh on both sides of slit to make pocket.
3. Stuff cavity.
4. Gently press edges together.

How to fillet a flat fish:

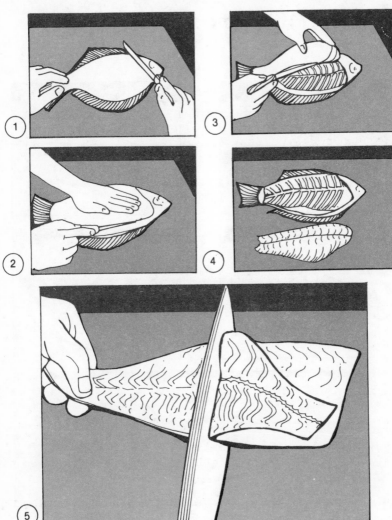

1 Make a cut behind pectoral fin just to backbone.
2 and **3** Slide knife along backbone under flesh until loosened.
4 Repeat on other side.
5 Remove skin by holding tail end, skin side down, and cutting through flesh as close to skin as possible.

How to split or butterfly:

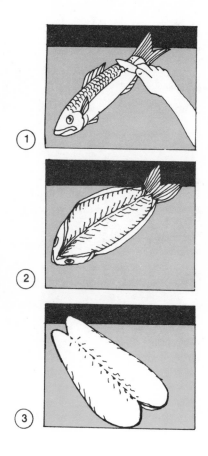

1 Clean and prepare fish as in How to Stuff a Round fish on page 25.
2 If barbecuing as a split fish, leave head and tail on.
3 For planked fish, remove fins, tail and head, leaving skin on and sides of fish joined along the back.

Saltwater Fish

Atlantic Croaker

(Corvina, Drum or Golden Croaker)

Croakers were abundant food fish about 25 years ago, but their numbers have steadily declined partly due to overfishing and climate changes. Now with the development of trawling in the Gulf of Mexico, croakers are reappearing in fish markets along the Atlantic coast.

A lean, white-fleshed fish, croaker ranges in size from 1/2 to 4 pounds; the smaller size makes an excellent pan fish, and the larger sizes are adaptable to any recipe. Croaker is available frozen and also as "flaked croaker," a frozen, precooked and breaded form which is becoming popular with American consumers.

Best cooking methods: baked, grilled, pan fried, poached.

FISH DIP

1 1/2 cups cooked, flaked croaker
1 cup sour cream
1 cup small curd cottage cheese
1/2 cup mayonnaise
1/2 cup grated carrot
1/4 cup grated onion
1/4 cup pickle relish
1 t prepared horseradish, or to taste
Salt to taste
Minced parsley

Combine all ingredients except parsley; chill well. Just before serving, garnish with parsley and serve with chips or raw vegetables.
Makes about 3 1/2 cups.

CROAKER SAUTÉ

1 1/2 lbs croaker fillets, or 4 small pan-dressed fish
1/2 cup flour
Salt and pepper to taste
4 T butter
Parsley sprigs and lemon wedges
Herbed Butter (recipe follows), or see page 215 for cold butter
    variations

Dust fish lightly with flour which has been seasoned with salt and pepper. Saute in butter over medium heat, allowing 10 minutes per inch of thickness at the thickest part; turn once. Test for doneness and serve with parsley, lemon and any cold herbed butter, which has been softened to spreading consistency.
Serves 4.

HERBED BUTTER

Cream 1/4 lb softened butter and add any of the following herbs, separately or in combination: 1 T minced parsley, 1 T snipped chives, 1 t dried tarragon.

Bluefish

Bluefish are delicious, feisty game fish found off the Atlantic coast from Florida to Nova Scotia. They range in size from 2 to 25 pounds; their season varies from December to April in southern waters and from May to October in northern waters.

The flesh of bluefish has a distinct flavor and a high oil content. The "fishiness" is most concentrated in the dark strips of meat on each side of the fish. The strips are easily removed by making shallow V-cuts the length of each fillet and lifting the strips out.

Fats and cooking oils should be used sparingly with bluefish; lime or lemon juice is good because it neutralizes the fish's natural oils. Bluefish generally does not make a good poaching or chowder fish because of its texture and oil content.

Best cooking methods: Snappers (baby bluefish, less than 2 pounds) are best when pan-dressed and pan fried whole. Bluefish weighing 6 to 8 pounds are used as steaks and fillets, baked, broiled or grilled. When grilling fillets, score on the skin side and cook them over a low fire, skin side down. Add wet hickory chips to the fire for added flavor. Bluefish weighing more than 10 pounds are baked whole and served chilled and skinless like a salmon. Hot-smoking methods are also good. Bluefish is well complemented by lemon or lime juice, white wine, onion, green pepper, oregano, tarragon, basil, garlic and tomatoes.

BAKED BLUEFISH IN WINE

2 small bluefish fillets, about 1 lb each, cleaned and dried
2 medium onions, thinly sliced
1/4 cup butter, softened
Salt and pepper; parsley, tarragon or dill
1/2 cup dry white wine
1/2 cup heavy cream
2 egg yolks, lightly beaten

Saute sliced onions in butter until soft, then use them to line bottom of greased baking dish which will hold fillets without overlapping. Lay fish on top of onions, dot with butter and sprinkle with salt, pepper and herbs. Add the wine and bake at 425°F, allowing about 10 minutes per inch of thickness at the thickest part of the fillet. Baste often and test frequently for doneness. When fish is cooked, drain liquids into a saucepan and keep fish warm. To the saucepan add cream and egg yolks and heat while stirring constantly until just thickened, but not bubbling. Correct seasonings and pour sauce over fish.
Serves 4-6.

BLUEFISH SALAD

3 cups cooked, flaked bluefish
1/2 cup salad oil
1/4 cup wine vinegar, or more to taste
2 T minced onion
2 T minced green pepper
2 t chopped parsley
1/2 t salt
1/4 t dried oregano
Dash garlic powder
Dash pepper
1/4 cup sour cream

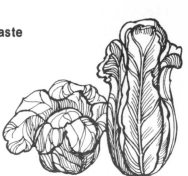

Romaine, Boston lettuce or other salad greens
Tomato and hard-boiled eggs, cut into wedges

Mix first 10 ingredients together except bluefish; let stand for 10 minutes. Gently mix in the flaked fish; chill. When ready to serve, stir in sour cream and serve on bed of lettuce; garnish with tomato and eggs.
Serves 4-6.

BLUEFISH IN SOUR CREAM

2 lbs bluefish fillets, cleaned and dried
Salt and pepper
1 cup sour cream
1/2 cup mayonnaise
1/4 cup grated Parmesan cheese
2 T chopped chives or 1 green onion, chopped
2 T lemon juice

Salt and pepper the fillets and place them in a large greased dish. Mix remaining ingredients together and spread over fillets. Bake at 350°F about 25 minutes or until fish flakes easily when tested. Place fish under broiler and continue cooking until sauce browns lightly.

Serves 4-6.

ORANGE-BROILED BLUEFISH

2 bluefish fillets, about 1 1/4 lbs each
Lemon or lime juice
1/2 cup frozen orange juice concentrate, thawed
1/4 cup butter, melted
1/4 cup soy sauce
1 T grated orange rind
Dash powdered ginger

Sprinkle cleaned and dried fillets with lemon or lime juice 30 minutes before cooking. Make an orange sauce by mixing the remaining ingredients together. Place fillets on greased rack of a broiler pan and baste generously with orange sauce. Broil 3 to 4 in. from heat, skin side down, for 10 to 15 minutes, depending on thickness of fish. Since the topping can become quite brown, you may wish to place fillets farther from heat and broil longer. For very thick fillets, when topping is brown, turn oven to 350°F and bake until fish is done. It is not necessary to turn fish during broiling or baking, but baste it often, testing for doneness with a knife point at the thickest part of the fish after 10 minutes.

Serves 4-6.

BAKED BLUEFISH IN CHIPS

2 lbs bluefish fillets, cleaned and dried
1/2 cup barbecue sauce, preferably homemade
1 large bag potato chips, crushed
Lemon or lime wedges

Cut fillets into serving-size pieces, dip in barbecue sauce and roll in crushed chips. Place the coated fillets in single layer in shallow, greased baking dish. Bake at 375°F, allowing about 12 minutes per inch of thickness at the thickest part of the fillet, until fish flakes easily. Garnish with lemon or lime wedges.
Serves 4-6.

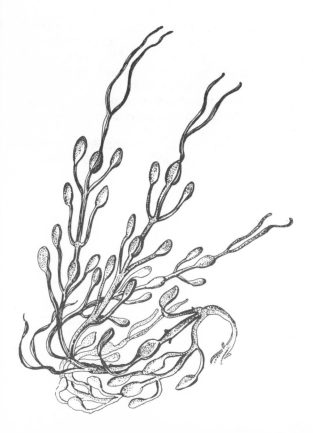

Cod

Cod is one of the most abundant and important fish families in the world; it includes haddock, pollock, hake (whiting) and freshwater burbot. Cod is primarily caught in New England waters and off the coasts of Newfoundland and Norway.

A lean, easily digestible, white-fleshed fish, cod lends itself to a variety of cooking methods and is complemented by rich sauces. All the fish in this family can be used interchangeably in most recipes.

Cod is marketed in a variety of sizes. The smallest is scrod, which is the designation given to both cod and haddock weighing between 1 1/2 and 2 1/2 pounds.

Codfish tongues and cheeks are also often found in the fish market; they are delicious when coated and fried or sauteed. The texture of the tongues is softer than that of the flesh, while the cheeks are firm, even after cooking. Many cooks prefer these fish parts for chowders and stews.

Salt cod is a dried form of cod which has been heavily salted to extract moisture and thereby preserve the fish. Before cooking, it must be soaked to remove the salt. The stiffer the fish, the longer the soaking time required. Soak in cold water for a minimum of 8 hours, drain the fish, cover it again with cold water and bring it gently to a boil. Skim off the foam, reduce the heat to a gentle simmer, and poach for 15 to 20 minutes, according to the thickness of the fish. When the fish is cooked, it can be flaked and used in your chosen recipe.

Best cooking methods: baked, broiled, sauteed, fried, stuffed.

COD BAKED IN HERBS

2 lbs cod fillets or steaks (haddock may be substituted)
1/2 cup butter
3 T soy sauce
1 clove garlic, minced
1/2 t basil
1/2 t rosemary
1/4 t tarragon
1/4 cup each sliced mushrooms and chopped green onions
Lemon slices

Place fillets or steaks in a greased baking dish. In a sauce-pan, melt butter; add soy sauce and herbs; pour over fish and bake at 375°F, allowing 10 minutes per inch of thickness at the thickest part of the fish. When almost done, remove fish from oven, sprinkle with mushrooms and onions and arrange lemon slices on top of fish. Make sure the topping is well basted with pan juices; return fish to oven and bake another 5 minutes, or until fish flakes easily and topping is heated through.
Serves 4-6.

CODFISH CROQUETTES

1 cup cooked, flaked codfish (prepared salt cod can be used)
1/3 cup chopped onion, sauteed in 1 T butter
1 1/2 cups Bechamel sauce, page 209
1 T minced parsley
Salt and pepper to taste (omit salt if using salt cod)
Oil for deep frying
Fine dry bread crumbs
1 egg, beaten
Egg Sauce, page 210, or Tomato Gravy, page 213

Combine fish, onions, Bechamel sauce and seasonings. When mixture is cool enough to handle, form into balls, 1 in. in diameter for appetizers, and 2 in. in diameter for main dish. Chill at least 1 hour. While oil in fryer or deep pan is heating to 375°F, roll codfish balls in crumbs, egg, then crumbs again, and fry until golden brown, about 1 minute for 1-in. balls and 2 minutes for 2-in. balls. Drain on paper towels and serve imme-diately with Egg Sauce or Tomato Gravy.
Serves 2 as a main dish, or makes about 12 appetizers.

CODFISH AU GRATIN

2 cups cooked, flaked codfish
1 1/2 cups Bechamel sauce, page 209
Salt
Dash cayenne pepper or Tabasco
1 cup grated, sharp cheese

Season Bechamel sauce to taste with salt and cayenne or Tabasco. In a greased 1 1/2-quart casserole, layer Bechamel sauce, half the fish and then half the cheese. Repeat layers, reserving some of the sauce to cover fish, then sprinkle with remaining cheese. Bake at 350°F about 1/2 hour, until browned and bubbling.
Serves 4.

SCROD FISHWICH

1 1/2 lbs scrod fillets, cut into 6 equal portions, well chilled
1 cup cornmeal
1/4 t garlic powder
1 t salt
1 t thyme
1 egg, beaten
Cooking oil
6 hamburger buns, toasted
Tomato, thinly sliced
Lettuce
Tartar sauce
Lemon wedges

Mix together the cornmeal and seasonings. Dip fish portions into egg and then seasoned cornmeal and refrigerate coated fish for 1/2 hour to prevent excess absorption of cooking oil. Pour 1/2 in. of oil into a heavy skillet and heat to about 370°F. Cook chilled fish until brown and crisp, turning if fillets are thick. Drain on paper towels. Serve on toasted hamburger buns with tomato slices, lettuce, tartar sauce and lemon wedges.
Serves 6.

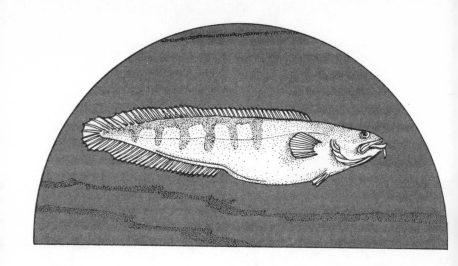

Cusk

A lean-white-fleshed fish found in the North Atlantic, cusk is most often marketed as fillets and may be prepared in the same way as haddock (page 48) or cod (page 40). Since it is a mild tasting fish, cusk is complemented best by seasonings and sauces. It is also a good chowder fish (page 193).

Best cooking methods: baked, broiled.

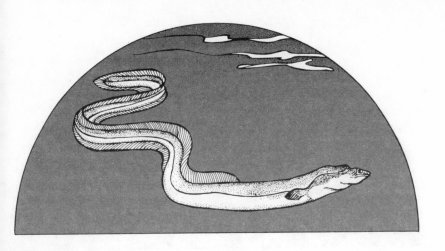

Eel

Eel is forever struggling to make itself known more widely in the United States. People who eat it can't say enough about it. People who have never tried it are reluctant to. In Europe and the Orient, eel is a prized fish which is consumed in significant quantities. In the United States, eel is often considered a delicacy and is hard to find outside big city fish markets. Perhaps if eels didn't so closely resemble snakes, we'd see them more often!

Smoked eel is a delicious appetizer. Most fish markets and specialty shops carry it or can special order it for you. Smoked eel will keep for several weeks, well wrapped, in the refrigerator, or longer in the freezer.

If you are fortunate enough to have access to fresh eel, you will discover it to be a rich, fat fish ranging in length from 10 to 16 in. If the eel is still alive, have your fish dealer kill, skin and clean it. If it is not alive, make sure it has a fresh odor and is free from slime. Uncooked eel will keep for 1 day in the refrigerator; cooked eel will keep for several days.

Eels are classified according to size: small, less than 1 pound; medium, 1 to 2 pounds; and large, 2 pounds or more. You should allow about 3 pounds of eel for six people.

Be adventurous. Go find an eel and treat yourself to a surprise!

Best cooking methods: sauteed, baked, broiled, fried, poached. Eel is complemented by fresh herbs. When using eel in a sauced dish, it helps to simmer the fish first for a few minutes in salt and vinegar to firm the flesh and remove excess fat.

EELS PROVENCALE

3 lbs eel, cleaned, skinned and cut into 2-in. pieces
2 quarts boiling water
1 t salt
1 1/2 t vinegar
Flour for dredging
Salt and freshly ground pepper
Butter
3 cloves garlic, minced
1/4 cup chopped fresh parsley

Parboil the eel in water with salt and vinegar. Cook for 2 to 3 minutes, then place eel in a colander and allow to drain well. When cool enough to handle, dredge eel in flour, salt and pepper. In a large skillet, saute eel in hot butter, turning often. Test for doneness with a knife point (a fork might cause flesh to break apart) and remove to a heated platter. Add garlic to the skillet and cook over low heat, adding more butter if needed. When garlic has softened, add the parsley and eel and toss gently to coat evenly. Serve eel with some of the garlic butter poured over the top.
Serves 6.

DEEP FRIED EEL

2 lbs eel, skinned, cleaned and cut into 1-in. pieces
1/2 cup evaporated milk, well chilled
1 t salt
1/8 t pepper
1/2 cup flour
1/4 cup cornmeal
Shortening or oil for frying
Tartar sauce

Dip eel into mixture of evaporated milk, salt and pepper, then dip into mixture of flour and cornmeal. Chill for 1 hour. Deep fry in oil at 360°F for 3 to 5 minutes or until fish flakes when tested with a knife point. Drain on paper towels and serve hot with tartar sauce.
Serves 4.

Note: Eel may be parboiled before dipping, as for Eels Provencale, above, to remove excess fat and firm the flesh. The frying time should then be reduced to 2 to 3 minutes.

SAUTEED EEL IN GREEN SAUCE

2 lbs eel, skinned, cleaned and cut into 1 1/2-in. pieces
2 quarts boiling water
1 t salt
1 1/2 t vinegar
Flour for dredging
Salt and freshly ground pepper
1/4 cup butter
1/2 cup chopped spinach, fresh; or frozen, thawed and
    uncooked
1/4 cup chopped fresh parsley
1/4 cup chopped green onion, green portion only
1/2 t dried tarragon
3/4 cup dry white wine
1/2 t salt
Dash cayenne pepper
2 egg yolks
1/4 cup heavy cream

Prepare eel as in Eels Provencale, page 45, except saute about 2 minutes, turn and cook 2 minutes more, adding spinach, parsley, onion and tarragon. Continue cooking for about 3 minutes, stirring constantly. Add white wine, cover and simmer for about 10 minutes. Remove pan from heat, remove eel and keep warm. Add salt and cayenne to pan and stir briefly. In a separate dish, beat egg yolks with cream, stir 1/4 cup of hot sauce into egg mixture and blend. Add egg mixture to sauce in pan, stirring gently until blended, then return to low heat and cook, stirring constantly, until sauce is thickened. **Do Not Let Boil.** Return eel to pan, stir to coat and heat gently. Serve eel with a generous amount of sauce.

Serves 4.

EEL BAKED IN CREAM

3 lbs eel, skinned, cleaned and cut into 3-in. pieces
2 quarts water
1 t salt
1 1/2 t vinegar
Lemon juice
2 egg whites, lightly beaten
1/4 cup flour
1/2 cup fine dry bread crumbs
1 t salt
1 t dried dill, or 2 T chopped fresh dill
1 small onion, minced
1/4 cup butter, softened
1 1/2 cups light cream

Parboil eel in water with salt and vinegar for 3 minutes. Remove eel to a colander and allow to drain well. When cool, sprinkle eel with lemon juice, dip into egg whites and roll in a mixture of flour, bread crumbs and salt. Place eel pieces in a buttered baking dish large enough to accommodate fish and sprinkle with dill and onion. Dot with 1/4 cup soft butter and bake at 375°F for 20 minutes. When eel starts to brown, add the cream and baste occasionally. Test with knife point for doneness.
Serves 6.

Note: When handling unskinned eels, it is advisable to wear gloves, or the eels' protective slime will adhere to your hands.

Haddock

Haddock, a member of the cod family, is one of the most important commercially caught food fish. It has lean, white, tender flesh that is high in protein and low in fat, is extremely versatile and can be substituted in any recipe calling for lean, white fish.

Haddock is most often sold as fresh or frozen fillets, although many fillets are frozen into blocks and processed into fish sticks and portioned convenience foods. Haddock weighing from 1 1/2 to 2 1/2 pounds is commercially marketed as "scrod." Although the price of haddock varies from season to season, it is available all year.

Best cooking methods: baked, broiled, sauteed, fried, stuffed.

HADDOCK A LA SECURITY

1 1/2-2 lbs small haddock fillets, cut into serving-size pieces
1/4 cup butter or margarine
1 1/2 cups Italian seasoned bread crumbs
1/4 cup grated Parmesan cheese
Seasoned salt
2 green onions, chopped
2 T chopped fresh parsley

In a nonstick skillet, melt butter or margarine. Coat fish pieces in a mixture of bread crumbs and cheese and cook over medium/high heat, a few minutes on each side. When fish is almost done, sprinkle lightly with seasoned salt, green onions and parsley and turn fish over to mix.

Serves 4-6 as a main dish.

Note: This makes a delicious appetizer or main course, served alone or with tartar sauce.

GRILLED HADDOCK KABOBS

2 lbs haddock steaks or fillets, 1 1/2 in. thick
1/4 cup lemon juice
1/4 cup lime juice
1/4 cup oil
1 or 2 cloves garlic, minced
1 t dried basil
1 t dried oregano
1 t salt
1/4 t pepper
2 sweet, red peppers, cut into 1-in. chunks
2 oranges, peeled and cut into chunks

Combine lemon juice, lime juice, oil, garlic and seasonings and mix well in a large glass bowl. Cut fish into 1 1/2-in. cubes and toss lightly in marinade. Cover loosely and let stand 2 hours at room temperature, mixing occasionally. Drain fish and dry, reserving half the marinade for basting, and heating the remainder in a saucepan.

Preheat broiler; thread fish onto skewers, alternating with red pepper and orange chunks. Place skewers on a rack which has been placed in a jelly roll pan (15 x 10 x 1 in.); broil 4 inches from heat. Turn one quarter turn every 2 minutes, basting with marinade, until fish flakes easily. Serve with reserved, heated marinade.

Serves 6.
Note: This fish can also be cooked on a grill, 5 inches from heat.

CHEESE BAKED HADDOCK

6 small haddock fillets, 1/3-1/2 lb each
Milk
6 T butter
Salt and pepper
1/3 cup chopped onion, sauteed in additional butter (optional)
6 slices white American cheese
1/2 cup Italian style bread crumbs

Roll up fillets and place in individual baking dishes. Add enough milk to half-submerge fish. Place 1 T butter in each dish, sprinkle fish with salt and pepper, add onion if desired and bake at 450°F for 6 to 8 minutes, basting often. Remove dishes from oven, place 1 slice of cheese on each, sprinkle with bread crumbs and bake another 5 minutes, until cheese is browned and fish flakes when tested with a fork.

Serves 6.

CEVICHE (Marinated Fish)

2 1/2 lbs haddock or halibut fillets
Juice of 6 limes
Juice of 6 lemons
2 tomatoes, peeled, seeded and chopped
2 red onions, thinly sliced
3 cloves garlic, minced
1/4 cup vegetable or olive oil
1/2 t hot red pepper flakes or 1/4 cup diced, canned green chiles
1/4 t dried oregano
Salt to taste
Lettuce
1 ripe avocado

Cut fish into 1/2-in. cubes, making sure all bones have been removed. In a glass bowl, combine fish cubes with juice from lemons and limes, making sure the fish is covered. Cover and refrigerate for 5 hours or overnight, stirring occasionally, until fish becomes opaque. Add remaining ingredients except lettuce and avocado, mix well, cover and refrigerate 1 hour more. Taste and add salt if preference dictates. Serve as an appetizer, on individual plates on beds of lettuce with avocado slices.

Serves 8-10 as an appetizer.

STUFFED HADDOCK PROVENCALE

2 haddock fillets, about 1 1/2 lbs each, skinned
Juice of 1/2 lemon
1/3 cup vegetable oil
1 large onion, thinly sliced
2 cloves garlic, minced
1 green pepper, finely chopped
1 4-oz can ripe olives, coarsely chopped
1/2 t salt
Freshly ground pepper to taste
3 T tomato paste
1 cup dry red wine
1 large tomato, thinly sliced
3 T chopped fresh parsley

Rinse fish and pat dry with paper towels; brush both sides lightly with lemon juice and set aside. In a medium-size skillet, saute onion, garlic and green pepper in oil until vegetables are limp but not brown. Add olives, salt and pepper and stir briefly to mix. Remove pan from heat and set aside. In a small dish, combine tomato paste and red wine; stir well and set aside.

Line a large baking pan with heavy aluminum foil; pour in half the tomato paste/wine mixture, spreading evenly with a spatula or pastry brush. Place one fillet on foil, skinned side down. Spread onion/garlic mixture evenly over fillet, then cover with tomato slices arranged in a single layer. Place second fillet on top and brush with remaining tomato paste/wine mixture. Wrap fish snugly in aluminum foil, adding a top sheet if necessary. Bake at 425°F, allowing 10 to 12 minutes per inch at the thickest part of both fillets, until fish flakes easily when tested. Sprinkle with fresh parsley and serve.

Serves 6-8.

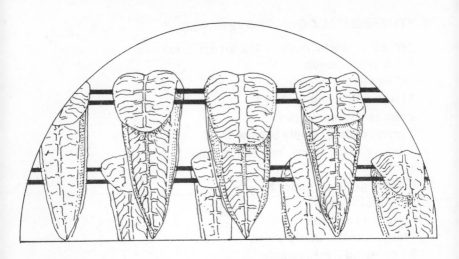

FINNAN HADDIE

The quality of finnan haddie varies greatly according to the freshness of the fish and the curing process. Look for a golden color and moist flesh with a delicate smoky flavor and a flaky texture. If finnan haddie is salty, dry and excessively fibrous, it is a poor product.

Smoked cod, halibut and pollock can be substituted for haddock. Flaked, cooked finnan haddie or other smoked fish can be used in any way you would use fresh cooked fish.

———————— ▶▸◆◂◀ ————————

FINNAN HADDIE CASSEROLE

1 1/2 lbs finnan haddie fillets (smoked haddock)
Milk or water
1 1/2 cups Bechamel sauce, page 209
4 hard-boiled eggs, coarsely chopped
2 cups mashed potatoes
Parmesan cheese

Poach fish in milk or water, enough to cover, allowing 10 minutes per inch of thickness at the thickest part of the fillet. Drain and cool fish; flake into large pieces, removing any bones. Add fish pieces and chopped hard-boiled eggs to Bechamel sauce and pour into a 2-quart casserole dish. Arrange the mashed potatoes around edge of dish, sprinkle with Parmesan cheese and bake in a hot oven (400°F) until top is browned.
Serves 4.

Hake

A member of the cod family, hake is a long, streamlined fish with a soft, white flesh which is more full-flavored than its other cod relatives. While some hake may reach 60 pounds, the average size is about 2 pounds.

In some cases, hake may be substituted for cod or haddock. It is not recommended for stews or chowders, however, since it becomes soft and falls apart.

Best cooking methods: baked, fried, corned, in fish cakes. Hake is well complemented by tomato- and onion-based sauces.

HAKE FISH CAKES IN TOMATO SAUCE

Good served with buttered noodles and a green salad.

1 lb hake fillets, finely cut
Tomato Sauce (recipe follows)
2 cups soft bread crumbs
1 small onion, grated
2 eggs, lightly beaten
1 T grated Parmesan cheese
1/2 t salt
Freshly ground pepper
1 t minced parsley, fresh or dried
Cooking oil and butter, equal parts

Prepare tomato sauce and let simmer for 20 minutes. Mix fish, bread crumbs, onion, egg, cheese and seasonings and form into balls, walnut-size or larger. Saute in oil or butter until brown, drain on paper towels and set aside. When all fish balls are browned, add to tomato sauce and simmer 10 minutes more.
Serves 4.

TOMATO SAUCE

1/2 cup chopped onion
2 cloves garlic, minced
2-3 T salad oil
1 1 lb, 12-oz can ground or chopped tomatoes
1 T sugar
Salt and ground pepper to taste

Saute onion and garlic in oil until soft but not brown. Add tomatoes, sugar, salt and pepper to taste. Simmer, uncovered, 20 minutes. Vary the sauce according to personal taste by adding wine, herbs, green pepper, etc.
Makes about 3 cups.

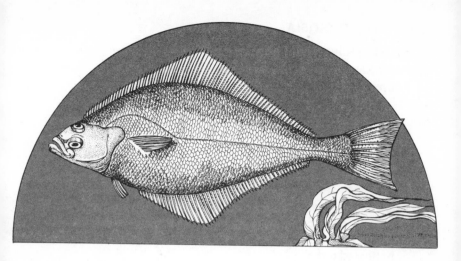

Halibut

The largest member of the flounder family, halibut can reach a weight of 600 pounds, although now it is rare to find one weighing 300 pounds. Halibut has a firm, white flesh with a delicate flavor. It is most often marketed as steaks.

Best cooking methods: poached, baked, broiled. Halibut is complemented by rich sauces. It is also good served cold in a salad or marinated raw as in Ceviche.

HALIBUT AMBROSIA

1 lb halibut fillets, cut into 1-in. cubes
Salted water
1/2 cup mayonnaise
1 T lemon juice
4 t grated orange rind
2 t sugar
1 cup celery, thinly sliced
1 cup fresh orange sections (peeled) or mandarin oranges
1/2 cup sliced ripe olives
1/4 cup sliced green onions with tops
1/4 cup shredded coconut (optional)
Lettuce or 2-3 whole pineapples, cut in half lengthwise and
hollowed out

Simmer fish cubes in salted water about 5 minutes, until fish flakes. Drain in colander and chill. Mix next 4 ingredients and chill. When fish is cold, toss with the next 5 ingredients, add the chilled mayonnaise mixture and mix lightly. Serve on a bed of lettuce or in pineapple boats.

Serves 4-6 as an appetizer or salad.

HALIBUT APPETIZER WITH DIPS

1 1/2 lbs halibut steaks, skinned and cut into 1-in. cubes
2 T soy sauce
Avocado Dip (recipe follows)
West Coast Dip (recipe follows)
Vegetable oil
6 T whipping cream
1/2 cup flour
Assorted raw vegetables
Chilled cooked shrimp or crabmeat

Toss cubed fish with soy sauce; cover and refrigerate, stirring occasionally, for 1 hour. Prepare the dips and set aside. In a large skillet, heat 2 inches of oil to 375°F. Drain fish and pat dry with paper towels. Dip the fish into cream, then flour, and fry by thirds until golden, about 2 minutes on each side. Drain on paper towels. Arrange the fish on a serving platter with the raw vegetables and shrimp or crabmeat; serve with the dips.

Serves 8-10.

AVOCADO DIP

1 large avocado, peeled and cut up
2 medium tomatoes, peeled, seeded and chopped
1/2 green pepper, seeded and chopped
4 oz cream cheese, softened
2 cloves garlic, cut up
1 t tomato paste
1 t salt
Dash cayenne pepper
Parsley sprig

Place all ingredients except parsley in blender or food processor and blend until smooth. Place in serving bowl and garnish with a sprig of parsley.
Makes 2 cups.

WEST COAST DIP

1/2 cup sour cream
1/4 cup mayonnaise
3 T minced mango chutney
2 T lime juice
2 T whipping cream
Lime twist or thin slice

Combine all ingredients except lime in a small bowl and mix well. Garnish with a lime twist or thin lime slice.
Makes 1 cup.

HALIBUT STEAKS WITH MUSHROOM STUFFING AND DILLED CUCUMBER SAUCE

4 halibut steaks, 1/2 lb each
1/4 cup chopped onion
4 T butter
1/2 cup sliced or chopped mushrooms
1/2 cup fresh bread crumbs
1/4 cup minced fresh parsley
2 T heavy cream
1/4 t thyme
Salt and freshly ground pepper to taste
1/4 cup melted butter
Dilled Cucumber Sauce (recipe follows)

Saute onion in butter until transparent. Add mushrooms, bread crumbs, parsley, cream and seasonings and mix well. In a well-oiled baking dish, place one steak, cover with stuffing and top with second steak, securing with toothpicks. Brush top with melted butter and season with additional ground pepper. Bake at 425°F, allowing 9 to 10 minutes per inch at the thickest part of both fillets, basting often with pan juices or with melted butter. Test for doneness with a fork; serve with Dilled Cucumber Sauce.

Serves 4-6.

DILLED CUCUMBER SAUCE

1 cup sour cream
1/4 cup mayonnaise
1 small cucumber, seeded and grated
1 T chopped green onion or chopped chives
1/2 t dried dill
1/2 t salt
1/4 t ground black pepper

Mix all ingredients well and refrigerate at least 1 hour before serving.

Makes 1 1/2 cups.

POACHED HALIBUT WITH ORANGE SAUCE

4 halibut steaks, 1/2 lb each, 3/4 in. thick
2 cups boiling poaching broth (see page 205),
    or 2 cups boiling water, plus 2 T lemon juice and 1 t salt
2 t cornstarch
1 T sugar
1 cup cold orange juice
2 t grated orange rind
1/2 t grated lemon rind
1 t lemon juice
2 oranges, skinless sections cut in half
1/4 cup raisins, soaked in hot water to soften

In a large oiled skillet, place steaks and boiling liquid. Cover and simmer until fish flakes easily, 8 to 10 minutes. Meanwhile, prepare sauce by mixing cornstarch and sugar in small saucepan. Add orange juice and heat slowly, stirring until thickened. Stir in orange and lemon rind, lemon juice, orange sections and raisins. Heat thoroughly. When fish is cooked, transfer carefully to rack to allow fish to drain. Serve on heated platter. Spoon some sauce over each steak and pass the rest.
    Serves 4.

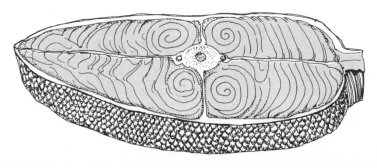

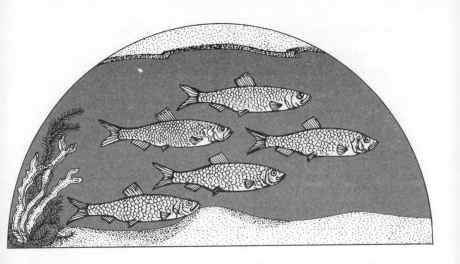

Herring

Herring has always been a commercially important fish and one of the ocean's most abundant species of fish. There is not great demand in this country for fresh herring, however; therefore we are more familiar with the preserved varieties, such as smoked, pickled, salted and kippered herring and sardines which are young herring from 2 to 3 inches long.

Herring may reach 18 inches in length (about 1 1/2 pounds in weight), but the common market size is between 9 and 11 inches. The fat content of herring varies between 5 and 15 per cent, depending on the time of year, the water temperature and the spawning season. Herring are the "fattest" when the water is warm and the fish are spawning.

If you are fortunate enough to have access to a packing plant or fish pier, you may be able to get herring directly from the boat.

If fresh herring is available, try them in the following recipes, or substitute fresh mackerel, which is similar in taste and texture. Some herring is also available fresh-frozen.

Because of the large number of bones found in herring, it is best in fresh herring recipes to use fillets no longer than 5 inches and to cook them at high heat, which helps to make the small bones soft and edible. It is always necessary to remove the backbone, regardless of the cooking method or size of the fish.

Best cooking methods: baked, pan fried, sauteed, broiled.

HERRING BAKED WITH CRUMBS

2 lbs small herring fillets, fresh or frozen
1/2 cup butter, melted
1 or 2 cloves garlic, minced
Oil
Salt and freshly ground pepper
3/4 cup dry bread crumbs
Lemon wedges

Remove dorsal (back) fin from fillets if necessary. Dip fillets into melted butter, in which garlic has been sauteed for 1 minute. Place the fillets, skinned-side down, in a well-oiled baking dish (15 x 10 x 1 in.). Sprinkle each fillet with salt, pepper and bread crumbs. Bake in a hot oven (500°F) for 10 minutes, or until fillets are brown and flake easily when tested. Garnish with lemon wedges.
Serves 6.

BAKED HERRING

2 lbs small herring fillets, fresh or frozen
Oil
1/3 cup soft butter
4 potatoes, thinly sliced
2 onions, thinly sliced and sauteed in additional butter
Salt and freshly ground pepper
Minced parsley
Lemon wedges

Oil a flat baking dish (15 x 10 x 1 in.) and arrange fish in the bottom skin side down. Dot fish with butter, cover with a layer of sliced potatoes, then a layer of onions. Dot with more butter and season with salt and pepper. Bake at 350°F until the potatoes are cooked, 30 to 40 minutes, basting from time to time with pan juices. Sprinkle fresh parsley on top and serve with lemon wedges.
Serves 6-8.

COLD HERRING APPETIZER

2 lbs small herring fillets, fresh or frozen
(see page 60 for size recommendation)
3 T olive or other vegetable oil
2 onions, chopped
4 medium tomatoes, peeled and chopped
2 cloves garlic, minced
1/2 t dried basil
1/2 t salt
Freshly ground pepper
1/4 cup tomato paste
Lettuce
Lemon wedges
Minced fresh parsley
Capers (optional)

Heat 3 T oil and saute tomatoes, onions and garlic until soft. Add the next 4 ingredients and simmer a few minutes. In an oiled baking dish, arrange fillets and top with tomato sauce. Cover and bake at 425°F for 10 to 15 minutes, or until fish flakes easily. Cool the fish in the sauce and refrigerate. Serve chilled on a bed of lettuce garnished with lemon wedges, parsley and capers (optional).
Serves 8-10.

MARINATED HERRING

The following recipes are for cooks who prefer to preserve their own fish without the addition of chemicals, dyes and excess salt. Experiment to find a marinade that suits your own tastes.

When marinating or pickling fish, use only glass, enamel or stainless steel utensils. Other metals may cause chemical reactions or add unwanted flavors. If jars with metal lids are used, insert several layers of plastic wrap between the jars and the lids to prevent the lids from corroding during storage. Leftover marinated herring will keep for several weeks in the refrigerator.

MARINATED HERRING

3 lbs fresh herring fillets, cut into 1-in. slices
3/4 cup distilled white vinegar
1/2 cup water
1/2 cup sugar
1 large red onion, chopped
1/2 t ground pepper
1/4 t salt
1 bay leaf, broken into quarters
6 whole allspice
1/2 t mustard seeds
1/4 t whole coriander

In a stainless steel or enameled saucepan, combine vinegar, water and sugar. Bring to a boil, reduce heat and simmer 2 to 3 minutes or until sugar has dissolved. Remove from heat and cool.

Rinse herring under cold water, then drain on paper towels. Place herring, onion and seasonings in a large glass bowl. Pour cooled marinade over all. Mix with a plastic or wooden spoon and pack fish down gently so marinade covers all surfaces. Cover tightly and refrigerate at least 24 hours. (It is best left refrigerated for 1 week.) This herring will retain its firmness and does not become soft like its commercial counterpart.

Serves 10-12 as an appetizer. Include onions from marinade with each serving of fish.

MARINATED HERRING WITH SOUR CREAM

1 recipe of Marinated Herring, above
1 cup sour cream

With slotted spoon, remove herring from marinade into a glass mixing bowl. Remove chopped onion from marinade and add to herring. Check glass bowl to see that you have 1/4 cup of marinade in bottom, adding more if necessary. Mix in 2/3 cup sour cream, folding gently. Taste and add more sour cream or more marinade until preferred taste is reached. Mix thoroughly and chill.

Serves 10-12 as an appetizer.

MARINATED HERRING WITH MUSTARD SAUCE

1 recipe of Marinated Herring, page 63
1/2 cup mayonnaise
1/3 cup sour cream
1/4 cup prepared mustard of your choice
1 T dried dill weed
Fresh parsley sprigs or fresh dill weed

Combine mayonnaise, sour cream, mustard and dill. Add drained herring pieces and chill. To serve, garnish with fresh dill or parsley sprigs.

Serves 10-12 as an appetizer.

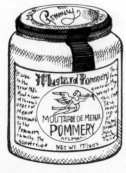

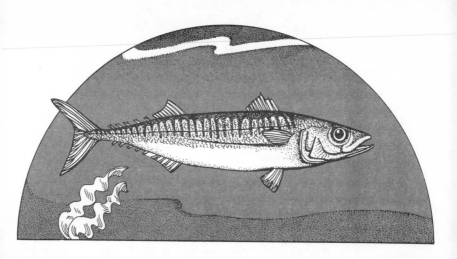

Mackerel

An abundant and important food fish, mackerel is found in both the Atlantic and Pacific oceans. The two types of mackerel most likely to be found in New England fish markets are Atlantic or Boston mackerel (1 1/2 to 2 1/2 pounds) and Spanish mackerel (2 to 4 pounds), which is one of the most delicately flavored members of the mackerel family. Both Atlantic and Spanish mackerel are marketed whole, dressed, filleted and steaked.

Mackerel has a firm fatty texture and may be substituted for bluefish, and vice versa, in most recipes. Mackerel tends to lose its flavor quickly when not iced or refrigerated immediately after being caught; however, it freezes well. (See Freezing, page 15.)

Best cooking methods: broiled, baked, grilled, smoked.

GRILLED MACKEREL

2 lbs mackerel fillets, unskinned
1/2 cup lemon juice
1/4 cup olive oil
1 t salt
1 or 2 cloves garlic, minced
1/2 t crushed rosemary
1/2 t freshly ground pepper

Wipe fillets with damp cloth and make 4 or 5 shallow slashes crosswise on skin side of each to prevent curling during grilling. In a shallow dish, marinate fish in remaining ingredients for 15 minutes on each side. Grill 4 inches from moderately hot coals, 5 minutes per side, basting with marinade. Test for doneness with a knife point. Placing fish in a hinged wire grill will help prevent fish from breaking when turned.

Serves 6.

BROILED BAHAMIAN MACKEREL A LA MORLEY

6 mackerel fillets, about 1/3 lb each
2 t salt
1/4 t each black pepper and cayenne
Juice of one lime
1/2 cup butter
1 medium onion, sliced very thin
6 thin slices bacon

Score mackerel fillets on the diagonal, making 1/2-in. deep cuts every inch, but taking care not to cut all the way through to the skin side.

In a small bowl, mix salt, black pepper, cayenne, and 1 to 2 t of the lime juice to moisten mixture. Spread mixture equally into the cuts, and on surface of fish if any is left. Sprinkle lime juice over each fillet and marinate, covered, for 2 hours in refrigerator. Preheat broiler; dot fish generously with butter, place onion slices on top, then one bacon slice lengthwise on top of each fillet. Broil about 10 minutes, depending on thickness of fish. Baste after 3 minutes with pan juices. Test for doneness with a knife point at thickest part of fillet.

Serves 6.

BAKED MACKEREL ESPAGNOLE

6 mackerel fillets, about 1/3 lb each, skinned
Tomato Sauce (recipe follows)
Oil and lemon juice for basting
1 1/2 cups soft fresh bread crumbs
3 T melted butter

Prepare Tomato Sauce and set aside. Oil fillets on both sides and brush with lemon juice. Place in a greased, shallow baking dish, skinned side down, and bake for 10 minutes at 350°F. Cover fish with tomato sauce and sprinkle with bread crumbs that have been tossed with melted butter. Bake for another 10 minutes or until fish is done and top is lightly browned.
Serves 6.

TOMATO SAUCE

1/4 cup olive or salad oil
3 cloves garlic, minced
1 onion, chopped
1 green pepper, chopped
1 1-lb can chopped tomatoes
1 8-oz can tomato sauce
Juice of 1 lime
1 t Worcestershire sauce
1 bay leaf
1/4 t dried oregano
Salt and ground pepper to taste
1 T sugar
2 T or more dry white wine

Saute garlic and onion in oil until soft but not browned. Add remaining ingredients and simmer, uncovered, until thickened (about 45 minutes), stirring occasionally.
Makes about 2 1/2 cups.

COLD MACKEREL DELIGHT

6 small mackerel fillets, about 1/3 lb each, skinned
Juice of 1 lemon or 2 small limes
3/4 cup flour
1/2 cup butter
1/3 cup vegetable or olive oil
2 cloves garlic minced
1/3 cup orange juice
4 green onions, chopped
2 T lime juice
Salt to taste
Dash Tabasco sauce
Lime wedges
Tomato, sliced
Avocado, sliced

Brush fillets with lemon juice, then coat with flour and saute in butter until golden. Place cooked fish in flat baking-serving dish. Combine next 7 ingredients in saucepan and simmer 5 minutes. Cool, pour over fish and refrigerate for 24 hours. When ready to serve, garnish with lime wedges and slices of tomato and avocado.

Serves 6 as a first course.

Ocean Perch

Ocean perch, also called redfish, rosefish or sea perch, is not a true perch, but a member of the rockfish family. Like its cousin the California rockfish, ocean perch has a firm, white, fine-textured flesh and a mild flavor. Of the 200 million pounds caught each year, most of the fish is marketed as frozen fillets, although fresh fillets are available.

Ocean perch is wonderfully versatile. Because of its mild flavor, it is well complemented by any kind of sauce from a simple herbed butter to a spicy tomato-based sauce. Ocean perch is also delicious served cold, accompanied by a tangy mayonnaise-based sauce.

There are usually six ocean perch fillets to a pound; allow two fillets per person unless you are serving heartier appetites.

Best cooking methods: sauteed, poached, broiled, steamed, fried.

OCEAN PERCH A L'ORANGE

2 lbs ocean perch fillets, skinned
Juice of 1 lemon
1/2 cup flour
Cooking oil/butter, equal parts
2 cloves garlic, minced
1/2 cup orange juice
1 T grated orange rind
1/4 t ground ginger (optional)
3/4 cup fish stock or water
2 t cornstarch mixed with 1 T cold water
Salt
Lemon juice
Sugar

Rinse fillets and pat dry with paper towels. Brush fillets with lemon juice and dust lightly with flour. In a large skillet, saute fillets in oil/butter until browned on both sides, about 3 minutes per side. Remove fillets to a heated serving dish and keep warm. Saute garlic in pan, adding more oil if necessary. Cook over low heat to prevent garlic from browning. Add the orange juice, orange rind, ginger and fish stock or water and simmer about 5 minutes. Add cornstarch mixture and stir over heat until thickened, adding more liquid if mixture is too thick. Season with salt, lemon juice and a little sugar if needed. Pour sauce over fish and serve.

Serves 6.

PERCH FRIED IN PAPER

Makes a delicious appetizer.

1 lb ocean perch fillets (flounder or bass may be substituted), cut into 12 equal pieces
Parchment, cut into 12 6-in. squares
Vegetable oil
Salt and ground pepper
Dry sherry
12 small strips of green onion
12 slices fresh mushroom
Grated fresh ginger
Peanut oil for frying
Chutney
Tartar Sauce
Curry powder

Brush paper squares with oil on one side only. Sprinkle fillets with salt, pepper and sherry. Place one piece of fish on each piece of oiled paper and top each with a strip of green onion, a mushroom slice and grated ginger. Fold paper in envelope fashion (see illustration). When all are folded, fry in 1 inch of oil heated to 370°F in a wok or deep skillet for 3 minutes or until lightly browned, turning once. Drain on paper towels and let each person open his own envelopes. Serve with chutney, or tartar sauce with a little curry powder added.
Serves 4 as an appetizer.

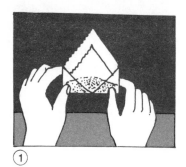 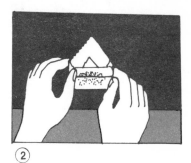

(1) (2)

1. With fish inside paper, fold diagonally, making sure bottom point is about 1 inch below top point. 2. Fold flaps to center, roll over once to form small envelope, then tuck upper flap inside to seal.

OCEAN PERCH PARMIGIANA

1 1/2 lbs ocean perch fillets, skinned
Lemon juice
Salt and freshly ground pepper
1 cup tomato sauce, homemade or canned
1 clove garlic, pressed through garlic press or finely minced
1/2 cup grated Parmesan cheese
2 T melted butter

Place fish in a shallow greased baking dish, brush with lemon juice and sprinkle with salt and pepper. Set aside. Add garlic to the tomato sauce, stir to blend and spread sauce over each fillet. Sprinkle with cheese and top with melted butter. Bake at 425°F until fish flakes when tested, about 15 minutes. If necessary, broil a minute to brown cheese.

Serves 4.

Note: Any sauteed vegetable, such as onions, mushrooms, or green peppers, can be added to the tomato sauce. Just simmer the mixture for 10 minutes before spreading the sauce over the fish.

Pollock

A member of the cod family, pollock is a lean, meaty fish with firm whitish grey flesh. Also known as Boston bluefish, pollock is an economical fish to buy during the winter, when it is most abundant along the New England coast.

This well-flavored fish is marketed mainly as frozen fillets under such names as ''ocean-fresh fillets'' or ''deep-sea fillets.'' Fresh pollock is sold drawn, dressed, filleted and steaked. It is an extremely versatile fish, wonderful in chowders (page 193) and a good substitute in any recipe for haddock (page 48) or cod (page 40).

Best cooking methods: baked, broiled, sauteed, fried, stuffed. Pollock is well complemented by rich sauces.

Red Snapper

The red snapper is the best known and most popular member of the large snapper family. Primarily fished with a hook and line, snapper is taken from the Gulf of Mexico, often from a depth of several hundred feet. The common market size is from 4 to 6 pounds and the lean meat is juicy, white and very flavorful.

Considered one of the most delicious deep sea fishes, snapper can be cooked by virtually any method in the manner of salmon as well as any lean white fish. The possibilities are practically unlimited.

Best cooking methods: baked, broiled, poached, grilled.

RED SNAPPER FILLETS AMANDINE

6 snapper fillets, 1/3-1/2 lb each
Salt and ground pepper
Flour for dredging
Butter
1/2 cup sliced blanched almonds
1/4 cup butter, melted
1 T lemon juice

Season fillets with salt and pepper, dredge in flour and saute in a skillet with butter, allowing 10 minutes per inch of thickness at the thickest part, and turning fillets carefully when half the cooking time is up. Remove cooked fish to a warm serving dish and add the almonds and butter to the skillet. Cook over low heat until the almonds are nicely browned; add lemon juice and pour sauce over fish.
Serves 6.

HEAVENLY SNAPPER

2 lbs snapper fillets, skinned
2 T lemon juice
1/2 cup melted butter
1/2 cup grated Parmesan cheese
1/4 cup butter, softened
1/4 cup mayonnaise
3 T chopped green onion
1/4 t salt
Dash Tabasco sauce

Brush fillets with lemon juice and refrigerate at least 10 minutes. Place fish on a well-greased broiler pan, brush with melted butter and broil about 4 inches from heat for 4 to 5 minutes. Turn fish carefully, baste again and broil another 4 to 5 minutes, until fish flakes easily. Combine Parmesan cheese with remaining ingredients and spread evenly over fish. Broil 2 to 3 minutes longer until lightly browned.
Serves 6.

Salmon

There is much to be said about the highly revered salmon. Even prepared in the simplest form, salmon is food for a gourmet. This sentiment was shared by cultures living as long ago as 25,000 B.C., when cave drawings and salmon bones gave visible evidence of the fishes' esteem.

The most important commercial species are chinook, coho and sockeye — all Pacific salmon — and the Atlantic salmon. Pacific salmon come from Alaska, the Columbia River in Oregon and the Puget Sound in Washington State. Atlantic salmon comes primarily from Canadian and European waters. Few Atlantic salmon are left in this country; some can be found in a few rivers in Maine, and some Maine lakes harbor land-locked salmon, which are fresh-water fish. Efforts are currently being made to restore this great species to United States waters.

Salmon range in size from 6 to 60 pounds or more, and the range in quality and texture is almost as great. The feeding habits of salmon greatly affect the quality and texture of the flesh. This applies to ocean-fed as well as land-locked salmon.

Spawning also adversely affects the quality of the fish. Since spawning fish do not eat, their flesh is generally watery and tasteless, since they draw off their own stores of fat and protein to sustain themselves.

Salmon are very versatile in the kitchen whether simply broiled or served with a rich sauce. For poached or baked salmon, center cut steaks are preferable; for broiling, the fatter cuts (those closer to the head) are best. Cold salmon is a wonderful summer dish; nothing is quite so impressive on a buffet table as a whole, chilled poached salmon. Just remember that careful cooking is important. Overcooked salmon is dry and tough.

Smoked Salmon. Here are just a few words on a sometimes confusing subject. Smoked salmon is a cold-smoked product; having first been brined and salted to draw out moisture, the salmon is then smoked for several days at temperatures ranging from 60° to 110°F. (The ideal temperature to prevent the growth of bacteria is 70°F.) If the salmon is then thinly sliced and covered with peanut or olive oil in an airtight container, it can be stored, refrigerated, for up to three months.

There are several different terms — mainly geographic distinctions — for Atlantic smoked salmon. They are Danish, Irish, Scottish, and sometimes Nova Scotia; the quality of each varies more from smokehouse to smokehouse than region.

Although some lox is salty, lox in general is the least salty, sweetest cure of all the smoked salmon; it is processed from Pacific salmon and is most popular in large Jewish communities. Prices vary according to the label, so beware. Let the quality and not the name be your guide.

Best cooking methods: broiled, baked, poached, grilled.

————————⯈•◆•⯇————————

HERBED BROILED SALMON

6 salmon steaks, 1/3-1/2 lb each
1 T juniper berries or green peppercorns
1/4 cup salad oil
Salt and ground pepper
Lemon wedges
1 cup mayonnaise
1 T chopped onion
1/2 t dried dill weed, or herb of your choice

Gently crush the juniper berries or peppercorns and press 6 to 8 berries into each steak. Brush steaks with oil and sprinkle with salt and pepper. Grill or broil fish about 5 minutes on each side, or 10 minutes per inch of thickness at the thickest part. Garnish with lemon wedges and serve with herbed mayonnaise sauce, made by adding the onion and herbs to the mayonnaise and allowing it to chill.

Serves 6.

POACHED SALMON WITH LEMON SAUCE

6 salmon steaks or fillets, 1/3 to 1/2 lb each
2 cups water
1 cup chicken broth
1/2 cup dry white wine
2 t minced onion
Lemon Sauce (recipe follows)
Dill weed

In a deep skillet 12 inches across or larger, bring water, broth, wine and onion to a boil and simmer a few minutes. Remove from heat and carefully lower fish into skillet. Return skillet to heat, bring back to boiling point and turn off heat. Simmer the fish until it flakes when tested, about 10 minutes per inch of thickness at thickest part. Remove carefully from skillet to a serving platter and keep warm, reserving broth. Prepare Lemon Sauce. To serve fish, spoon some sauce over each piece, sprinkle with dill weed, and pass the rest of the sauce.
Serves 6.

LEMON SAUCE

3 T butter
3 T flour
1 1/4 cups poaching liquid
1/2 cup heavy cream
1 t salt
3 T lemon juice
Dash ground pepper

Melt butter in a small saucepan and stir in flour. Cook over low heat until bubbling. Remove from heat, stir in poaching liquid and cream. Return to heat and cook until slightly thickened. Add remaining ingredients, adjust seasonings and serve.
Makes 2 cups.

SALMON MOUSSE
WITH CUCUMBER AND SOUR CREAM SAUCE

2 cups cooked salmon, chilled
1 1/2 T unflavored gelatin
1/2 cup cold water
3 T lemon juice
1 T chopped onion
1/2 cup mayonnaise
1/2 t dried dill weed
1/4 t paprika
Dash salt and Tabasco
1/2 cup chopped celery
1 cup light cream
Oil
Lettuce leaves
Parsley sprigs
Cucumber and Sour Cream Sauce (recipe follows)

In a small saucepan, sprinkle gelatin over cold water, place over low heat and stir until gelatin dissolves. Remove from heat and cool. Into blender container, pour gelatin and lemon juice and blend about 30 seconds. Add onion, mayonnaise, dill, paprika, salt, Tabasco, celery and salmon; blend well. Add cream and blend again until mixture is smooth. Oil a 4-cup mold — a fish mold if you have one — and fill with salmon mixture. Cover and chill several hours until set. To unmold, dip mold in warm water, wipe dry and invert quickly onto a bed of lettuce leaves arranged on a large platter. Garnish with fresh parsley sprigs and serve with Cucumber and Sour Cream Sauce.
Serves 8.

CUCUMBER AND SOUR CREAM SAUCE

1 cup sour cream
1/2 cup mayonnaise
1 small cucumber, peeled and chopped
1 small green onion, finely chopped
Salt and pepper to taste

Combine all ingredients and refrigerate at least 1/2 hour to allow flavors to develop. Serve with Salmon Mousse.
Makes 2 cups.

SALMON STUFFED WITH WILD RICE

1 whole dressed salmon, 4-5 lbs, prepared to stuff, see page 25
2/3 cup chicken broth
1/3 cup packaged wild and brown rice mixture
1 small onion, finely chopped
4 large mushrooms, chopped
2 T butter
2 T lemon juice
1/2 t dried dill weed
1/8 t ground pepper
1/4 cup vegetable oil mixed with 2 T melted butter
Lemon wedges
Mushroom Sauce (recipe follows)

In a small saucepan, bring chicken broth to a boil; add rice and simmer, covered, until rice is tender, about 30 minutes. Set aside. Saute the onion and mushrooms in butter in a medium-size skillet until liquid evaporates, about 6 minutes. Stir in rice, lemon juice, dill weed and pepper. Stuff fish with the rice mixture and sew closed.

Place fish in an oiled, shallow oven-to-table baking dish or pan and brush all over with oil. Cover head and tail loosely with foil and bake at 350°F for 45-60 minutes, basting frequently, until fish flakes easily when tested. Carefully remove top skin and serve each portion with a lemon wedge, or with Mushroom Sauce.

Serves 8.

MUSHROOM SAUCE

3 T butter
1 T minced onion
1/2 cup sliced mushrooms
3 T flour
1 1/2 cups half and half cream
1/2 cup sour cream
Salt to taste

In a saucepan, saute onions and mushrooms in butter until tender. Stir in flour, cook briefly, then add half and half and cook over medium heat until thickened, stirring constantly. Remove from heat, stir in sour cream and salt to taste.

Makes about 2 1/2 cups.

SALMON SALAD WITH PINEAPPLE

Great as a cool summer lunch.

1 1/2 cups cold cooked salmon in chunks
1/2 cup fresh or canned pineapple chunks
3/4 cup chopped celery
3 green onions, chopped
1/4 cup mayonnaise
Salt to taste
Lettuce leaves
1 small cucumber, thinly sliced and marinated in French
　　dressing

Combine the salmon, pineapple, celery, onions and mayonnaise and mix lightly, adding salt if needed. Cover and chill until ready to serve. Mound salad on lettuce leaves and garnish with cucumber slices.
Serves 4.

Sea Bass

Sea bass, or black sea bass, is a popular and delicious gamefish with firm, white flesh. Its delicate flavor is attributed to a rich diet of shrimp, crab and other shellfish.

Sea bass is suited to any cooking method. It is extremely popular in Chinese restaurants where it is often used for whole, steamed or fried fish. At the fish market, the average size of a whole fish is between 1 1/2 and 5 pounds. Sea bass is also available filleted or steaked.

Best cooking methods: baked, steamed, deep fried, sauteed.

CHINESE SEA BASS WITH SWEET AND SOUR SAUCE: TWO METHODS

Method 1: Steamed

2 lbs sea bass fillets, skinned
4 T soy sauce
2 t white wine vinegar
1/4 cup oil, preferably peanut
1/4 cup chopped green onion
Boiling water
Sweet and Sour Sauce (recipe follows)

Prepare Sweet and Sour Sauce and keep warm. Arrange fish fillets in a single layer in a shallow oven-proof baking dish. Combine soy sauce and vinegar and sprinkle evenly over fish. Repeat process with oil and onions. Place a rack in the bottom of a large roasting pan with a cover, and pour in just enough boiling water to cover rack. Place the baking dish on the rack, bring water back to a boil, cover and steam over moderate heat until fish flakes easily, 10 to 15 minutes. When fish is cooked, remove roasting pan from heat and uncover, allowing steam to escape. Carefully lift platter from pan (it will be very hot). Drain juices from platter and serve fish with warm Sweet and Sour Sauce.
Serves 6.

Method 2: Fried

2 lbs sea bass fillets, skinned
Peanut oil for deep frying
Cornstarch, sifted
Sweet and Sour Sauce (recipe follows)
Chopped green onion

Prepare Sweet and Sour Sauce and keep warm. Heat oil to 360°F in a pan deep enough to cover fillets. Dredge fish in cornstarch and fry at one time only as much fish as will easily fit into pan without overlapping. It may be easier to cut fillets in half before cooking. Cook 5 to 8 minutes, depending on thickness of fish. Always bring oil back to cooking temperature before adding next batch of fish. Drain fish on paper towels and keep warm. When all fish is cooked, serve immediately with the warm sauce. Garnish with chopped green onion.
Serves 6.

SWEET AND SOUR SAUCE

1 cup pineapple juice
1/3 cup distilled white vinegar
1/4 cup brown sugar
1 T soy sauce
1 small green or red pepper, seeded and chopped
1/2 cup fish stock or chicken broth
1 t grated ginger root or 1/2 t ground ginger
1 T cornstarch mixed with 1/4 cup cold water
2 slices canned pineapple, cut into small chunks

Bring all ingredients except cornstarch mixture and pineapple to a boil in a saucepan and simmer 1 minute. Add cornstarch mixture and cook until thickened, stirring constantly. Add pineapple, heat and serve sauce over fish.
Makes 2 1/2 cups.

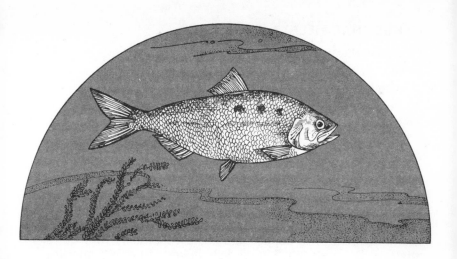

Shad

American shad is a member of the herring family, but because of its importance it deserves a section of its own. Spring is the season for this fatty, delicate fish, since it leaves the ocean to spawn in rivers, much like salmon. The female shad is considered the most desirable, as the fillets are larger and fatter than those from the male. Shad range in size from 1 1/2 to 8 pounds.

Because of shad's unusual bone structure, filleting the fish yourself can be tricky. Have your fishmonger do it for you or have him teach you if you want to learn for yourself.

Best cooking methods: baked, sauteed, broiled.

BAKED SHAD FILLETS

2 lbs shad fillets, boned, skin on
Juice of 1/2 lemon
1/4 cup butter
2 T vegetable oil
2 cloves garlic, minced
2 T chopped green onion
Ground pepper
Chopped fresh parsley

Brush fillets with lemon juice. Melt butter and add oil, garlic and onion; heat briefly. Brush bottom of baking dish lightly with butter mixture and arrange fillets in dish, skin side down. Sprinkle with pepper and baste generously with butter mixture. Bake at 450°F until fish flakes, 10 to 12 minutes. Sprinkle with fresh parsley and serve.

Serves 4-6.

SHAD FILLETS AMANDINE

2 lbs shad fillets, boned
Salt and ground pepper
Flour for dredging
3/4 cup milk
1 cup dry bread crumbs
1/4 cup butter
1/2 cup blanced, slivered almonds
Juice of 1/2 lemon

Make sure all bones have been removed from fillets. Season fillets with salt and pepper and dredge in flour. Dip in milk, then in bread crumbs and brown in butter over moderate heat. Reduce heat and cook, allowing 10 minutes per inch of thickness at the thickest part. When half-cooked, turn gently and cook until fish flakes easily. Drain on paper towels and place on heated platter. In same pan, brown almonds, adding more butter if necessary. Add lemon juice to almonds and pour mixture over fish.

Serves 4-6.

SHAD ROE

Shad roe is considered a great delicacy and is excellent sauteed, baked or broiled. Roe bought at the fish market will be cleaned and ready for cooking. (1 1/2 pounds of roe will serve 6.) If you catch your own fish, remove all blood clots, veins, slime and the outer membrane from the roe, leaving the inner membrane intact. Wash thoroughly.

Fresh roe should stand in ice-cold salted water for a few minutes, then be simmered until it firms, 4 or 5 minutes. It can then be cooled, dredged in flour and sauteed in butter over low heat. If desired, you can add herbs such as dill or tarragon to the pan. When the roe has browned, serve it with the drippings from the pan and garnish it with parsley sprigs and lemon wedges. Do **not** overcook; the roe will become tough.

Shark

If you were playing word association games and someone said "shark," most people would say "jaws," not "grilled," "broiled" or "teriyaki." Reputations are hard to live down, but personalities aside, shark is a delicious lean fish. Mako is probably the most popular shark, although dogfish is the primary ingredient for the English "fish 'n chips."

The smaller the shark, the more tender it is. Marinades add flavor as well as tenderness. Some cooks feel it necessary to soak shark in brine (1 cup of salt to 1 gallon of water) for several hours before cooking to neutralize any residual ammonia and firm the flesh. If the fish has been properly handled at the market, however, soaking shouldn't be necessary.

Use care not to overcook shark. It should be moist, not dry. Since the texture of the flesh suffers greatly from freezing, use fresh shark whenever possible.

Be inventive! Shark is a versatile and economical food.

Best cooking methods: baked, poached, fried, grilled.

OVEN-FRIED SHARK

2 lbs shark fillets or steaks, cut into serving-size pieces
1/2 t salt
1/2 cup light cream or half and half cream
1 cup dry bread crumbs
1/4 t ground pepper
1/4 t dried basil
1/3 cup butter, melted
Tartar sauce

Mix salt with cream, dip shark into liquid and roll in bread crumbs which have been mixed with pepper and basil. Arrange fish in a well-greased baking dish and drizzle melted butter evenly over each piece. Bake at 500°F for 10 to 12 minutes, or until fish flakes easily. Serve with tartar sauce.

GRILLED SHARK STEAKS ORIENTAL

2 lbs shark steaks, cut into serving-size portions
1/4 cup orange juice
1/4 cup soy sauce
2 T ketchup
2 T oil
2 T chopped parsley
1 T lemon juice
2 cloves garlic, minced
1/2 t dried basil
1/4 t ground pepper

Arrange fish in a single layer in a shallow baking dish. Combine remaining ingredients and pour over fish. Let stand for 30 minutes, turning fish once. Remove fish from sauce, saving sauce for basting. Grill shark about 4 inches from moderately hot coals for 6 minutes. Baste, turn and cook 6 minutes longer, or until fish flakes easily.
Serves 6.

SHARK TERIYAKI

2 lbs shark fillets, cut into 1-in. chunks
1 16-oz can pineapple chunks
1/2 cup soy sauce
1/4 cup dry or sweet sherry
2 T brown sugar
1 t grated ginger root or 1/2 t ground ginger
1 t dry mustard
2 cloves garlic, crushed
1 green pepper, seeded and cut into 1-in. squares
Cherry tomatoes, parboiled mushrooms, pearl onions and
      summer squash chunks
Metal skewers
Hot cooked rice

Drain pineapple, reserving 1/4 cup juice. Combine pineapple juice, soy sauce, sherry, brown sugar, ginger, mustard and garlic and pour over fish chunks in a glass dish. Cover and chill at least 1 hour, stirring occasionally. Drain fish chunks and reserve marinade. On skewers, alternate fish chunks, pineapple and vegetables as desired. Cook over hot coals or 4 inches from broiler for 5 minutes, basting with marinade. Turn and cook another 5 minutes or until fish flakes easily. Serve on a bed of rice.

Serves 6-8.

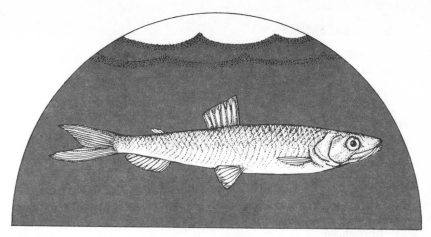

Smelt

Smelt is a small, "smooth and shining" (the meaning of the Anglo-Saxon word "smoelt"), silvery fish which averages in size from 6 to 8 inches. Unless you are fortunate enough to participate in a "smelt run," when the fish enter the rivers to spawn, you will find smelt in the market whole, drawn or pan-dressed, fresh or frozen. Like most oily fish, the quality of fresh smelt deteriorates quickly, so freshest is best. If the smelt have picked up an unpleasant flavor from the river or are excessively oily, it is best to throw them out.

The most poular way to cook smelt is to fry them, either in the pan or in deep fat. Boning small smelt is more a matter of taste than necessity; boning large fish is necessary, and it's easier when they're cooked. The fish can be split to shorten cooking time. Generally speaking, it takes 10 to 12 smelt, or one pound, to feed two people. Buy more if appetites are large.

Cleaned and gutted smelt can be frozen by inserting them, head end first, into a plastic freezer container and filling it to the top with water. When frozen, seal the container with several layers of aluminum foil and an elastic band. Frozen this way, the fish should last up to 6 months.

Best cooking methods: pan fried, deep fried, sauteed.

DEEP FRIED SMELT

2 lbs smelt, cleaned
Flour for dredging
1 egg beaten with 1 T water
Dry bread crumbs
Oil for deep frying
Tartar sauce

Dip smelt into flour, then into egg mixture, then into bread crumbs. Refrigerate while you heat oil to 375°F. Deep fry a few fish at a time; do not crowd them. Allow 2 to 4 minutes cooking time, depending on size of fish. Drain on paper towels and serve with tartar sauce.

Serves 4-6.

SWEDISH SMELT FRY

2 lbs small- to medium-size smelt
1 2-oz can anchovy fillets
1/4 t salt
1/8 t pepper
1/2 cup flour
3 T butter
3 T cooking oil
Buttered rye bread
Sliced tomatoes
Sliced cucumbers
Lemon wedges
Anchovy-Dill Sauce, heated (recipe follows)

Remove fish heads, and clean fish if whole. Drain anchovies, saving oil for sauce. Cut anchovies in half lengthwise and place half inside each smelt. Sprinkle smelt with salt and pepper and roll in flour. In a large skillet, heat butter and oil until bubbly, then cook fish until crisp, about 2 minutes each side. Drain on paper towels and serve with buttered rye bread, sliced tomatoes and cucumbers, lemon wedges and warm Anchovy-Dill Sauce.

Serves 4.

ANCHOVY-DILL SAUCE

2 T minced onion
Reserved anchovy oil
1 1/2 T flour
1/2 t salt
1 1/3 cups half and half cream
1 egg yolk, beaten
1 T lemon juice
1/2 t dried dill weed

Saute onion in oil until tender, blend in flour and salt, stir in cream and cook until thickened, stirring constantly. Add a little of the heated sauce to egg yolk in a small bowl; then, while stirring, add this mixture to remaining sauce, heating until thickened. Remove from heat and add lemon juice and dill.

Makes 1 1/2 cups.

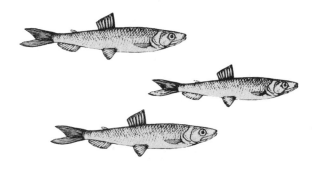

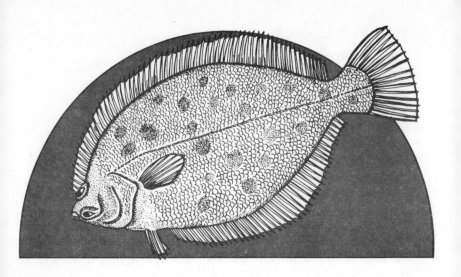

Sole

No other fish but sole can be prepared in such a variety of ways, or is so well suited to the accompaniment of sauces, spices, fruits, vegetables and other fish and shellfish.

Unfortunately, there is no true Dover sole in American waters. Authentic Dover sole is found in European waters from the Mediterranean to Denmark, and comes to us frozen and expensive. What we buy in the local fish market as fresh ''sole'' is actually one of a number of species of flounder. The following are native to our Atlantic waters: **winter flounder,** marketed as lemon sole when weighing more than 3 pounds and as blackback when less than 3 pounds; **American plaice,** the Atlantic variety often marketed as sanddab (not to be confused with the Pacific variety named Pacific sanddab); **Atlantic halibut,** the largest of the flatfish family; and **summer flounder,** also known as fluke.

These are just a few of the names used for flounder. If the fish is fresh and you enjoy it, that's what counts. Prices vary as much as the names, so ask questions and obtain the best deal.

Since the size of fillets differs so much, allow 1/2 pound per person to be safe. Be careful not to overcook sole; it is delicate and cooks quickly. Create your own dishes and enjoy them!

Best cooking methods: baked, stuffed, broiled, fried, sauteed, poached.

DANISH SOLE WITH CURRY

3 lbs sole or flounder fillets
1/2 cup flour
1 cup butter
2 T lemon juice
1 T chopped parsley
1/4 t salt
2 t mild curry powder
1 t Worcestershire sauce
2 T ketchup
1 T chutney
3 large apples, peeled, cored and cut into 1/2-in. slices
1 1/2 cups Bechamel sauce, heated, page 209
Hot parsley potatoes (optional)

Dust fillets lightly with flour. In a large skillet, melt 1/2 cup of the butter; add lemon juice, parsley and salt and cook for 1 minute. Add fish and saute until browned and fish flakes easily when tested (allow 10 minutes per inch of thickness at the thickest part). Remove pan from heat and keep warm.

In another skillet, melt remaining 1/2 cup of butter. Add curry powder, Worcestershire, ketchup and chutney and cook over medium heat for 3 minutes, stirring constantly. Cook apple slices in curry mixture until tender but not overly soft; keep warm. To serve, arrange fillets, overlapping them slightly, on a large, hot platter. Place slices of apple around fish and pour heated Bechamel sauce over fish. This is wonderful with parsley potatoes.

Serves 6-8.

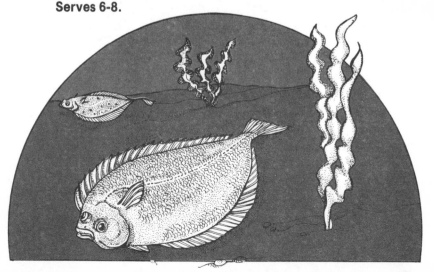

NUTTY PARMESAN SOLE

2 lbs sole or flounder fillets
1/2 cup butter, softened
1/2 cup grated Parmesan cheese
1/2 cup chopped macadamia nuts
Salt to taste
Lemon wedges

Thickly spread 1/4 cup of the butter on the bottom of a shallow baking dish. Sprinkle with 1/4 cup cheese and arrange sole fillets on top in a single layer. Dot fish with remaining butter, sprinkle with rest of cheese and chopped nuts. Bake at 400°F about 10 minutes, basting often, until nuts are browned and fish flakes easily when tested. If desired, place under broiler to brown tops of fish. Serve with pan juices over fish; salt lightly and garnish with lemon wedges.
Serves 4-6.

ALMOND-FRIED FLOUNDER

2 lbs (10-12) small sole or flounder fillets
2 eggs, beaten
3 T cornstarch
2 T dry white wine
1 t Worcestershire sauce
1/2 t salt
1/4 t pepper
1 1/2 cups blanched almonds, coarsely ground
8 strips cheddar or Swiss cheese, 2 in. x 1/2 in.
4 green onions, minced
8 5-in. wooden skewers
Vegetable oil for deep frying

Mix eggs with the next five ingredients. Dip fish pieces into egg mixture and roll fish in nuts. At narrow end of each fish piece, place a strip of cheese and 1 t onion. Roll up, starting at narrow end, and secure with a wooden skewer. Chill 15 minutes. Heat oil to 375°F and fry rolls 3 to 4 minutes, until golden. Drain on paper towels.
Serves 4 generously.

FLOUNDER ILENA

2 lbs small sole or flounder fillets
3 T butter
1/2 cup finely chopped onions or shallots
Salt and ground pepper
Flour
1/3 cup dry white wine or vermouth
1 egg, beaten with 1/2 cup whipping cream
1 1/2 T chopped fresh parsley
1/2 t dried basil
1 T lemon juice
Salt to taste
Lemon wedges

In a skillet, saute onions in butter over low heat until soft; do not brown. With a slotted spoon, remove onions to oven-proof baking dish. Sprinkle fish with salt and pepper, coat lightly with flour and saute in same skillet, adding more butter as needed. Cook over medium heat about 2 minutes on each side. Layer fish over onions in baking dish; keep warm.

In same skillet, add the wine and cook over high heat for 3 minutes, scraping sides and bottom of pan. Remove skillet from heat, let cool briefly, then, while stirring constantly, pour a little of the pan juices into the egg/cream mixture, to which the parsley and basil have been added. Return the mixture to the pan and cook over very low heat, stirring constantly until thickened, 2 to 3 minutes. Beat in lemon juice and salt and pour sauce over fish in baking dish. Place under preheated broiler for about 1 minute, until sauce begins to brown. Garnish with lemon wedges.
Serves 4-6.

CHINESE FLOUNDER WITH ONION AND PEPPERS

1 1/2 lbs flounder or sole fillets, cut across grain into 1 1/2-in.
   strips
1/2 t grated fresh ginger
2 T soy sauce
1/2 t sugar
1 T vegetable oil
2 T dry or sweet sherry
1 egg, lightly beaten
1/4 cup cornstarch, sifted
7 T oil
1 thin slice fresh ginger
1 clove garlic, crushed
1 small red pepper, cut into strips 1 in. x 1/4 in.
1 small green pepper, cut as above
1 medium onion, thinly sliced
1 T sweet or dry sherry
1 T soy sauce

Combined grated ginger and next 4 ingredients in a glass bowl; add fish strips, toss to coat and marinate for 2 hours, stirring occasionally. Dip fish pieces into egg, then cornstarch and set aside.

Heat 2 T of the oil in a wok or skillet and saute ginger and garlic until golden; remove and discard. Add peppers and onions to same oil and stir fry for 2 minutes; don't brown. Stir in sherry and soy sauce; remove vegetables and sauce and keep warm.

Heat remaining 5 T of the oil in same pan until hot; add fish and fry quickly on both sides until brown. Drain on paper towels and serve on warm platter; garnish with reserved onions and peppers.

Serves 4.

SOLE PARMESAN WITH TOMATO SAUCE

2 lbs sole or flounder fillets, 1 lb each, cut in half
Salt and ground pepper
Flour
2 eggs, beaten
3/4 cup dry bread crumbs, plain or Italian-style
1/2 cup grated Parmesan cheese
Dash cayenne pepper
2 T butter and 2 T oil
Chopped fresh parsley
Tomato Sauce (recipe follows)

Season each fillet with salt and pepper. Dust with flour, dip into egg, and dip into mixture of bread crumbs, cheese and cayenne, coating well. Refrigerate for 15 minutes. Heat butter and oil in a large skillet and cook fish until browned on both sides, allowing 10 minutes per inch of thickness at thickest part. Test for doneness with a fork. Serve with chopped fresh parsley and Tomato Sauce.
Serves 4.

TOMATO SAUCE

1 onion, thinly sliced
2 T butter
2 T flour
1 1/2 cups stewed tomatoes
Salt and pepper
2 t sugar
Dash ground ginger
1 bay leaf

Saute onion in butter until pale golden brown. Add flour to pan and cook, while stirring, until flour bubbles. Add remaining ingredients and heat to boiling. Reduce heat and simmer 20 minutes.
Makes about 1 1/2 cups.

BAKED FLOUNDER WITH ORANGE SAUCE

2 lbs flounder or sole fillets, 1 lb each, cut in half
1/2 cup frozen orange juice concentrate, thawed
1/2 t salt
Dash ground pepper
2/3 cup corn flake crumbs
1/4 cup butter, melted
Orange Sauce, heated (recipe follows)

Combine orange juice concentrate, salt and pepper, dip fish into orange juice mixture and roll in crumbs. Place fish in a single layer in a shallow, well-greased baking pan and drizzle melted butter evenly over fish. Bake at 500°F for 10 to 15 minutes, depending on the thickness of the fish. Fish is done when it flakes easily when tested. Serve fish with warm Orange Sauce.
Serves 4-6.

ORANGE SAUCE

2 T white wine vinegar
2 t sugar
1/2 cup chicken broth
1/4 cup frozen orange juice concentrate, thawed
1/4 cup water
1 T grated orange rind
1/4 dry white wine
1 T cornstarch

Bring vinegar and sugar to a boil in a 1-quart saucepan; boil until sugar begins to caramelize and turn brown. Be careful not to burn. Remove from heat and add chicken broth; return to low heat and simmer for 1 minute, stirring constantly, until caramel is dissolved. Add orange juice concentrate, water and orange rind. Mix wine and cornstarch and add to pan; stir constantly until mixture has thickened.
Makes 1 1/4 cups.

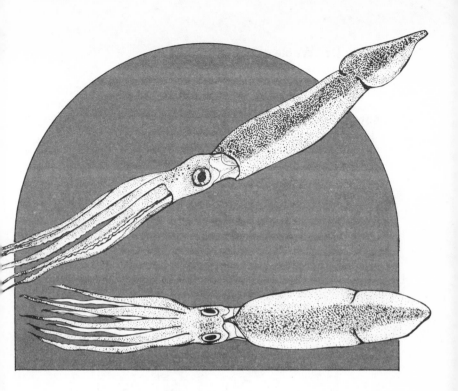

Squid

Squid, like octopus, belongs to the mollusk family. Unlike its relatives, scallops, clams, and oysters, squid wears its shell internally in the form of a long, semi-rigid "pen" or "quill," which helps to support its body. Squid has the ability to change color while alive, but in the market, it is usually a mottled light pinkish purple.

The United States market for squid is growing as people become aware of its versatility in the kitchen. It is high in protein, easily digestible, inexpensive and relatively easy to prepare.

Whole squid is available fresh or frozen. The average market size is from 10 to 12 inches in length; the smaller size is superb for deep frying while the larger size is perfect for stuffing. The flavor and texture of squid are delicate, and care should be taken not to overcook squid or it will become tough and rubbery. Generally speaking, allow 1 pound of squid for 2 to 3 servings.

Best cooking methods: baked, baked-stuffed, fried.

If the squid has not already been cleaned at the market, you can do it yourself with reasonable ease (see page 102).

Method 1: Use Whole or in Rings

A. Thaw the frozen squid under running water. Cut through the arms near the eyes. With your thumb and forefinger, squeeze out the inedible beak between the arms. Reserve the tentacles.

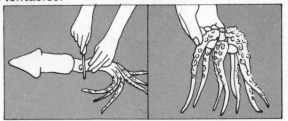

B. Feel inside the mantle for the pen or quill; grasp it firmly and pull. The pen should pull out with the viscera attached; discard. Wash the mantle thoroughly to remove any ink; drain. The squid is now ready for stuffing. For rings, cut across the mantle. The tentacles can be chopped, minced or left whole.

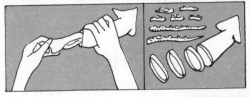

Method 2: Use as Strips and Pieces

A. Repeat as in Method 1, step A
B. Repeat as in Method 1, step B

C. To cut strips or pieces, lay the mantle flat and cut down the center from top to tail. Spread open and wash thoroughly.

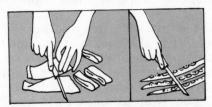

D. Cut the mantle into whatever size strips or pieces are desired. The arms can be chopped, minced or left whole.
Note: Check to see if the speckled membrane covering the mantle has been removed; if not, pull it off and discard.

BAKED STUFFED SQUID I

18 small fresh or frozen squid, thawed
2 15-oz cans marinara sauce
2 7-oz cans minced clams
1 bay leaf
1/2 cup thinly sliced green onions with tops
1 lb ricotta or cottage cheese
1/4 cup dry bread crumbs
1/2 t dried oregano
1 T chopped fresh parsley
1/2 cup thinly sliced celery
1 egg
Salt to taste
6 oz Mozzarella cheese, sliced
Hot cooked spaghetti

Clean and prepare squid as in Method 1; drain well and set aside. In a saucepan, mix marinara sauce and liquid from clams; set clams aside. Add the bay leaf and 1/4 cup of the green onions to the sauce; bring to a boil. Reduce heat and boil gently, uncovered, until thickened, about 30 minutes, stirring often.

In a bowl, mix ricotta, bread crumbs, oregano, parsley, celery, egg, clams and the rest of the green onion. Blend well and season to taste with salt. Stuff squid hoods (mantles) with cheese mixture, using your fingers or a small spoon. Do not overstuff, since squid will shrink during cooking. Fasten the open ends of the hoods with toothpicks to prevent stuffing from spilling out. Arrange stuffed hoods in a shallow 3-quart baking dish and top with body-leg sections. Pour sauce over all and bake, uncovered, at 400°F for 20 minutes. Top with Mozzarella slices and bake about 5 minutes longer, until cheese melts. Serve squid and sauce over individual servings of hot spaghetti, allowing about 3 squid per person.
Serves 6-8.

BAKED STUFFED SQUID II

12 medium squid, cleaned and prepared as in Method I
1 cup ground beef
1/2 cup fresh bread crumbs
1 cup cooked rice, white or brown
2 cloves garlic, minced
Salt and ground pepper to taste
1/2 cup grated Romano cheese
1/2 cup raisins
2 T minced fresh parsley
1/2 t dried oregano
2 cups spaghetti sauce, canned or homemade

Saute ground beef until all traces of pink have disappeared; drain off fat. Add bread crumbs, rice and garlic to meat, toss and saute 1 minute. Season with salt and pepper. Cool mixture slightly and add Romano cheese, raisins, parsley and oregano. Stuff squid with mixture, being careful not to overstuff as the squid will shrink slightly during cooking. Secure open ends with toothpicks and place in one layer in a well-greased, shallow baking dish. Pour spaghetti sauce over all and bake at 350°F for about 30 minutes, until squid is tender. Allow 2 squid per person.

Serves 6.

FRIED SQUID

This is an easy way to become acquainted with squid. Use small squid, from 6 to 8 inches long; it will be more tender. If only larger squid is available, cut into thinner rings and pieces.

1 to 2 lbs fresh or frozen squid, thawed
Garlic salt
1 part dry bread crumbs to 1 part flour, about 1 cup total per pound of squid
Vegetable oil
Tartar Sauce

Clean and prepare squid as in Method I. Cut mantle crosswise into 1/4-in. rings. Drain squid of excess water and sprinkle with garlic salt. Coat rings and bodies (with legs attached) with the mixture of bread crumbs and flour; shake off excess. In a deep saucepan, heat 1 1/2 inches of oil to 375°F. Cook rings one spoonful at a time for about 30 seconds, or until lightly browned. Squid becomes very tough if overcooked. Drain rings and keep warm. Bring oil back to 375°F before adding more squid. Cook bodies and legs last, 30 to 45 seconds. They tend to spatter, so keep a lid or splatter screen handy. Serve at once with tartar sauce.
One pound serves 2-3.

Striped Bass

Like salmon, striped bass is a saltwater fish that reproduces in fresh water rivers. This popular and exciting gamefish, known as "rockfish" around Chesapeake Bay, is most common from Cape Cod to South Carolina, although "stripers," as they are also known, almost annually venture into Maine waters, causing great fervor among fishermen. Stripers weighing between 30 and 70 pounds have been landed by rod and reel. The best market size for the kitchen, however, is from 6 to 8 pounds. The heavier the fish, the coarser the flesh. The larger fish are more suited to flaked dishes or broiled steaks.

When caught by sportsfishermen, striped bass should be gutted and iced as soon as possible to preserve its freshness and quality. It also deserves mention that striped bass, like smelt, picks up off-flavors of water that is not pure and clean; therefore, open ocean fishing is the best guarantee of good quality.

Striped bass has a white, flaky flesh that is moderately fatty and is adaptable to almost any method of cooking. Striped bass is also complemented by aromatic sauces. If striped bass is not available, red snapper can easily be substituted in all the following recipes.

Best cooking methods: broiled, baked, poached, oven fried, sauteed.

STRIPED BASS IN PARCHMENT

This method of cooking is nowhere near as complicated as some think, and the results are wonderful.

1 1/2-2 lbs striped bass fillets or 6 individual steaks, skinned
1 1/2 cups Bechamel sauce, page 209
2-3 T sweet sherry
2 egg yolks
1/4 cup chopped mushrooms
1/4 cup chopped onions or 2 shallots, chopped
2 T butter
1/2 cup chopped, cooked shrimp or crabmeat
Salt and ground pepper
Parchment, enough to make 6 pieces, each 8 in. x 11 in.
   (see Note)

Add sherry to Bechamel sauce and cook for 1 minute over low heat; remove sauce from heat and beat in egg yolks. Return to low heat and cook until smooth and hot. Stir in mushrooms and onions that have been sauteed in butter until soft. Add shrimp or crabmeat, cover and set aside.

Cut fillets into 6 equal pieces, each to fit on half the parchment with enough border left to fold the edge over twice. For each envelope, place some of the sauce in the center of half the parchment, place fish portion on top, sprinkle lightly with salt and pepper, then add more sauce to cover fish. Fold parchment over the fish and secure edges so that no steam can escape. Place the 6 envelopes on a large baking sheet and bake at 425°F for 10 minutes per inch of thickness at the thickest part of the fish, plus 5 minutes more for the parchment. When cooked, slide each envelope onto a platter or individual serving plates and cut open with scissors. Serve with any remaining warm sauce.
   Serves 6.
   Note: Parchment is thin, unglazed paper similar to onion skin, which prevents loss of moisture and retains juices during cooking. It is available at most gourmet kitchen supply shops.

STRIPED BASS WITH CRABMEAT STUFFING

1 whole striped bass, 3-4 lbs, dressed, rinsed, dried and
    prepared to stuff, see page 25
1 onion, chopped
1 stalk celery, chopped
3 T butter
1 cup fresh bread crumbs
7 oz crabmeat, fresh and flaked (pick over well to remove any
    shells)
1/4 cup milk
Salt and ground pepper
1/4 cup lemon juice
3 T butter, softened
Lemon wedges

Saute onion and celery in butter until soft. Add bread crumbs and saute for 1 minute. Stir in crabmeat and enough milk to make a moist stuffing. Season to taste with salt and pepper.

Into the cavity of the whole fish, sprinkle 2 T of the lemon juice, spoon in the stuffing and close the opening with small skewers or wooden picks. Wrap the head and tail with aluminum foil and place the fish in a large, well-greased baking pan. Spread soft butter over exposed portion of fish and sprinkle with remaining 2 T of lemon juice. Bake at 400°F, basting every 10 minutes. Cook about 45 minutes, or until fish flakes easily when tested at the thickest part. When fish is cooked, carefully remove top skin and serve each portion with a lemon wedge.

Serves 6-8.

BROILED STRIPED BASS FLAMBE

**2 lbs striped bass fillets, cut into 6 equal servings;
   or 6 individual steaks**
1/3 cup butter, melted
Lemon juice
Salt and ground pepper
1 T dried fennel or fennel seeds
1/4 cup brandy or cognac, warmed
Lemon wedges

Rinse fish or wipe with damp cloth; dry well with paper towels. Place fish on oiled broiler rack, brush with melted butter and sprinkle with lemon juice. Lightly salt and pepper, and broil, allowing 10 minutes total cooking time per inch of thickness (a 1-inch steak = 5 minutes on each side), turning steaks and thick fillets when half-cooked. Baste with butter and lemon juice and cook until fish flakes. Thin fillets will break if turned, so they can be cooked on one side until done. When fish is done, carefully place on heat-proof platter on which you have placed 2 t of the dried fennel. Sprinkle remaining fennel on top and pour warmed brandy over all. Carefully ignite brandy and allow it to burn out; serve with lemon wedges.
Serves 6.

Swordfish

Swordfish is found in waters worldwide and is popular despite its high price. When prices are very high or swordfish is scarce, mako shark can be successfully substituted. Mako is comparable in quality and texture and much lower in price.

Swordfish is marketed fresh and frozen, primarily as steaks. It has a moderate fat content and a firm, delicious flesh. It is especially well-suited to grilling and broiling and gains added flavor by marinating and/or using pungent herbs and spices, such as curry, garlic, oregano and basil. You can serve swordfish with sauces, but it is so good by itself that you should try it alone first, then decide. Be careful not to overcook this fish; it should be moist, not dry.

When broiling or grilling make sure swordfish steaks are from 3/4 to 1 inch thick. Steaks that are too thin may dry out and thicker steaks will not cook all the way through before the outside is overdone.

Best cooking methods: baked, broiled, grilled.

GRILLED MARINATED SWORDFISH I

6 swordfish steaks, about 1/2 lb each and 1 in. thick
1 cup vegetable oil
Juice of 1 lemon
4 cloves garlic, minced
2 T dried basil
1 T dried oregano
1 t celery salt
1/2 t ground pepper
1/2 cup butter, melted
Minced fresh parsley

Combine oil, lemon juice, garlic, herbs and salt and pepper; mix well. Brush both sides of fish generously with the mixture and refrigerate in marinade for 2 hours. Turn steaks every half hour to marinate thoroughly. Grill about 6 inches from coals for 5 minutes; turn, baste and cook 6 or 7 minutes more. Serve steaks brushed generously with melted butter and topped with fresh parsley.
Serves 6.

GRILLED MARINATED SWORDFISH II

4 swordfish steaks, about 1/2 lb each
1/2 cup orange juice
1/4 cup salad oil
1/4 cup soy sauce
1/4 cup ketchup
2 T lemon juice
2 cloves garlic, minced
2 T minced fresh parsley
1/2 t dried oregano
Freshly ground pepper
Lemon wedges

Combine all ingredients except fish. Marinate fish in the mixture in the refrigerator for 2 hours, turning once. Broil or grill fish, basting often with marinade, until done, 5 to 6 minutes per side. Serve with lemon wedges.
Serves 4.

SWORDFISH SAUTEED WITH ROSEMARY

4 swordfish steaks, about 1/2 lb each
Flour
2 t crushed rosemary
Vegetable oil
5 T butter
Salt and pepper to taste
1/4 cup dry white wine or dry vermouth
Lemon wedges

Lightly dredge fish in flour and work rosemary into flesh with fingers. Brush fish with oil and saute in butter over moderate heat 5 to 6 minutes per side. Place fish on a warm platter and sprinkle with salt and pepper. Add a little more butter to the pan and add wine. Heat through and pour over fish. Garnish with lemon wedges.

Serves 4.

Tilefish

Despite its unusual name and odd appearance, tilefish is beginning to find its way into American kitchens. It is a lean fish with very firm yet tender flesh, similar in texture to lobster and scallops. A versatile white fish, tilefish can be grilled or smoked and is complemented by herbed butters and sauces.

In the market, tilefish ranges in size from 6 to 8 pounds, although it can grow to 50 pounds. It is in the low to medium price range and is most plentiful in the winter months. It deserves a turn in your kitchen; you may be pleasantly surprised!

Best cooking methods: broiled, baked, deep fried, poached, chowdered.

INDIVIDUAL TILEFISH QUICHES

This makes a good first course or a delicious luncheon dish with a lettuce, cucumber, onion and orange salad.

1 1/2 lbs tilefish fillets, cooked and flaked
Water or milk, lightly salted
1/4 lb Swiss cheese, grated
6 individual pie shells, 3-4 in. diameter
2 whole eggs plus 2 egg yolks
2 cups light cream or half and half cream
1 t minced onion
1 T minced green pepper
Salt and pepper to taste
2 T dry or sweet sherry

Poach fish in enough lightly salted water or milk to cover; cook until tender. Drain, flake and toss with cheese. Place fish mixture in bottom of pie shells. Mix remaining ingredients well and cook over moderate heat until warm. Pour over fish in pie shells and bake at 425°F for 15 minutes; reduce heat to 325°F and bake 15 minutes more.
Serves 6.

TILEFISH WITH BROILED SPINACH TOPPING

1 1/2 lbs tilefish fillets, cut into 6 equal pieces
Lightly salted water
2 packages frozen chopped spinach, cooked
1 small onion, finely chopped
1/4 cup sour cream
1/4 cup mayonnaise
1/2 cup grated Parmesan cheese
1 egg yolk, beaten
2 t lemon juice
Salt and pepper to taste

Poach fish pieces in salted water until almost done, 6 to 8 minutes. Drain. Place fish in a well-buttered baking dish. Drain cooked spinach and press out extra liquid; mix in remaining ingredients (reserving 1/4 cup of the Parmesan cheese) and spread over fish. Sprinkle with remaining 1/4 cup cheese and broil until browned and bubbling.
Serves 6.

TILEFISH SPREAD

1 lb tilefish fillets (any lean, firm white-fleshed fish may be used)
2 cups boiling water
1 rib celery, cut into pieces (leaves too)
1 bay leaf
1/2 t salt
1/2 cup mayonnaise
1/2 cup Thousand Island dressing
1/2 cup chopped celery
1/2 small red onion, chopped
Crackers or chips

To boiling water, add celery, bay leaf and salt. Add fish and simmer gently until tender, 8 to 10 minutes. Drain and chill fish, then flake and mix well with the next 4 ingredients. Chill for 1/2 hour to let flavors blend. Serve with your favorite crackers or chips.
Makes 2 cups.
Note: To make an attractive serving mold for dips, freeze some pretty seashells in plain water in a ring mold. Turn the mold out onto a platter which will catch the melting water. Place a bowl of any cold dip in the center of the mold and garnish with parsley or thin lemon slices.

CHILLED TILEFISH AND FRUIT SALAD

1 1/2 lbs tilefish fillets
Lightly salted water
1 large, ripe avocado
2 cups orange sections, cut in half if large
2 T orange juice
1 T lemon juice
1 cup sliced celery
1/2 cup mayonnaise
1/2 cup slivered almonds, toasted
Assorted salad greens

Poach fillets in salted water for about 8 to 10 minutes, until tender. Drain, cool and break into large chunks. Cut avocado into 1-in. pieces and toss with orange sections, orange juice and lemon juice. Add celery, mayonnaise, almonds and fish; chill well. Serve on individual plates on beds of greens.
Serves 6.

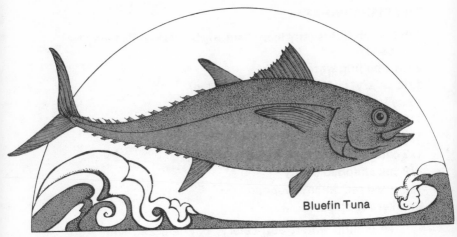

Bluefin Tuna

Tuna

There is definitely more to tuna than casseroles, salads and sandwiches. Tuna has been an important fish food for centuries; it was utilized by ancient cultures in Greece, Peru and Japan. Today, tuna is a primary seafood in this country, although the majority of the catch goes to processing plants. Canned tuna may be popular, but more people are discovering fresh tuna and are finding out what a delicious source of high-quality protein, vitamins and minerals it is.

The most common species of tuna found on the United States market are albacore, bluefin and yellowfin tuna. Albacore, found in both the Atlantic and Pacific oceans, is the most important tuna in the domestic canning industry, the lightest fleshed of the tunas and the only one that can be labeled as ''white meat'' in canned products.

Bluefin, the largest tuna family, is found primarily in the Atlantic Ocean. The flesh of bluefins weighing more than 120 pounds is dark, but the smaller bluefins are canned as ''light meat'' tuna.

Yellowfin, the major catch for the California canning industry, has flesh which, when cooked, is darker than albacore but lighter than bluefin. Yellowfin is canned as a ''light meat'' product and is the tuna generally used in ''fancy'' products.

The meat of the tuna varies not only in color but in fat content, depending upon spawning season and diet. Tuna is fattest prior to spawning and leanest after. Generally speaking, the lighter the flesh, the more delicate the flavor and texture.

The type of fresh tuna most commonly found along the northeastern coast of the United States is the bluefin. Its flesh is medium to deep red, similar to raw beef, with a firm texture and rich flavor.

When preparing fresh tuna, it may be necessary before cooking to remove the dark midline strip of flesh which is oily and can be bitter after cooking. It may also be necessary to soak the fish in brine to remove any residual blood. Add 1 cup of salt to 2 quarts of water and soak the fish in this brine in the refrigerator for 1 hour. Tunas usually requiring brining are the larger bluefin, bonito and skipjack. Brining isn't necessary with the small bluefin, albacore, blackfin and yellowfin tuna.

Best cooking methods: broiled, grilled, baked.

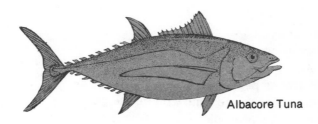

Albacore Tuna

CANNED TUNA

Tuna is canned in three styles: solid or "fancy," chunks or "standard," and salad "flaked" or "grated." All styles come packed in oil, or brine (salted water), which is more expensive.

Solid or "fancy" usually means large pieces of solid meat. This type is best used in dishes or salads calling for large chunks. Chunks or "standard" usually contains three pieces of solid meat per 7-ounce can, with small flakes of fish added to give the desired weight. It is the moderately priced style and is good for casseroles. Salad "flaked" or "grated" is in the form of small crumbs and is the least expensive product. Usually packed at the same time as "fancy," "flaked" quality is just as good as the more expensive packs. It is best for use in salads and sandwiches.

The quality of canned products depends on the type of tuna used. Albacore, with its white meat, is considered the best. In order of decreasing desirability are tunas packed as "light meat," which could be yellowfin or little bluefin, and "dark meat," which applies to the larger (more than 120 pounds) bluefin or skipjack tuna.

If you have a pressure cooker, you can make your own "canned" tuna. Clean and soak the tuna steaks as necessary. Check cooker directions or add 2 inches of water to the cooker, bring to a boil and add the fish. Cover and cook for 20 minutes under full (15 pounds) pressure. The meat will be in tender chunks when done and can be frozen in pan juices for future use. Chilled, the tuna can be used in salads, sandwiches or any way you would use regular canned tuna.

SALAD NICOISE

3 7-oz cans white tuna in oil, or same amount fresh cooked tuna
1 2-oz can flat anchovy fillets, chopped
3/4 cup chopped celery
2 cloves garlic, minced
1/4 cup chopped onion
1/4 cup chopped green pepper
1 t chopped fresh thyme
1 bay leaf, broken
1/2 t rosemary
2 T red wine vinegar
7 T olive oil
Salt and ground pepper to taste
4 ripe tomatoes, skinned and cut into wedges
14 pitted black olives, sliced
4 hard-boiled eggs, cut into quarters
1 red onion, sliced into thin rings

Soak anchovy fillets in water to remove some of the salt. Drain the tuna and cut into chunks. Combine tuna, anchovies, celery, garlic, onion, green pepper, thyme, bay leaf and rosemary in a bowl; toss gently. Add wine vinegar, oil and salt and pepper. Gently toss again; then carefully fold in tomatoes, olives and hard-boiled eggs. Chill. To serve, garnish with onion rings.
Serves 8.

GRILLED FRESH TUNA

4 individual tuna steaks, about 1/3 lb each and 1 in. thick
3 T olive or vegetable oil
1 or 2 cloves garlic, pressed
2 T tarragon vinegar or lemon juice
Freshly ground pepper
Hot garlic butter, page 214

Marinate tuna steaks in olive oil mixed with garlic and vinegar for about 1 hour. Grill over charcoal or under the broiler, allowing 10 minutes per inch of thickness at thickest part, basting often with marinade and turning once during cooking. When tender, season with pepper and serve with garlic butter.
Serves 4.

Yellowfin Tuna

GOLD COAST OMELET

Good accompanied by a lettuce and fresh fruit salad.

**2 7-oz cans tuna in water, drained and flaked, or equal amount
   of fresh cooked tuna**
2 cups half and half cream
2 T sliced green onion
1/2 t dried thyme
2 T dry sherry
Dash cayenne pepper or Tabasco
2 or 3 T minced fresh parsley
2 T flour
1/4 cup water
12 eggs
Dash ground pepper
1/4 cup butter
1 1/2 cups grated cheddar cheese

In a saucepan, heat the drained tuna, cream, green onion, thyme, sherry, cayenne and parsley until hot. Blend flour with water until smooth; add to sauce, stirring constantly, and cook until thick. Cover and keep warm.

For each omelet, beat 2 eggs and dash pepper together. Melt some of the butter in a skillet, add eggs and cook omelet until almost done. Sprinkle 1/4 cup grated cheese on top and cook until cheese melts. Remove omelet to warmed platter, place 1/2 cup tuna mixture on half the omelet and fold other half over it. Keep warm, and repeat 5 more times.
   Serves 6.

TUNA WITH TOMATO ASPIC

2 7-oz cans tuna, drained and flaked, or equal amount of fresh
  cooked tuna
1/2 cup mayonnaise
1 1/2 T chopped chutney
1/2 t curry powder
1 cup chopped celery
4 hard-boiled eggs, chopped
3 T chopped onions or scallions
1 T lemon juice
Tomato Aspic (recipe follows)
Salad greens
Parsley sprigs

Prepare tomato aspic; chill until firm, several hours or overnight. Mix the mayonnaise with chutney and curry powder; then add tuna, celery, eggs, onion and lemon juice. Blend well but gently, and chill. When ready to serve, unmold Tomato Aspic onto serving platter. Mound tuna mixture in center and surround aspic with salad greens. Garnish tuna with parsley sprigs.
Serves 6-8.

TOMATO ASPIC

2 cups tomato juice
2 bay leaves
1/4 cup each chopped onion and celery
5 whole peppercorns
6 to 8 whole cloves
Dash cayenne pepper
1 t horseradish
2 T unflavored gelatin
1/2 cup cold water
1/2 cup orange juice

Cook tomato juice, bay leaves, onion, celery, peppercorns, cloves, cayenne and horseradish until vegetables are soft. Strain and force through a sieve. Soften gelatin in cold water and stir into tomato mixture, heating until gelatin dissolves. Cool, stir in orange juice and pour mixture into a lightly oiled 4-cup ring mold or 6-8 individual ring molds. Chill until firm, several hours or overnight. Unmold by dipping bottom of mold in warm water to loosen. Pat dry and turn out onto serving platter. Fill with chilled tuna or any seafood salad.
Serves 6-8.

HOT TUNA ROLLS

2 7-oz cans tuna, drained and flaked, or equal amount fresh
    cooked tuna
3 T lemon juice
4 T any type pickle relish/pepper relish
1 cup chopped celery
2 T minced fresh parsley
2 T chopped green onions
2 T chopped green pepper
Mayonnaise
Ground pepper
4 hot dog buns
4 slices cheddar cheese
Parchment, cut into 4 pieces, each large enough to enclose a
    hot dog bun (see Note)

Mix tuna thoroughly with lemon juice, relish, celery, parsley, onions and green pepper; add enough mayonnaise to
moisten well. Add pepper to taste. Open hog dog buns carefully (do not break apart) and gently scoop out the soft inner
part, leaving the shell. Divide tuna equally among buns and
place a slice of cheese lengthwise on top of each. Wrap in
parchment or butcher's paper, folding so that seam is on the
top. Bake at 400°F on a baking sheet for 6 to 8 minutes. Tuna
should be heated through, cheese melted and buns crisp. Serve
in the wrappers.
Serves 4.
Note: Parchment is available through most specialty food
shops. Its purpose is to retain moisture while heating the food
inside. Unglazed butcher's paper or small brown paper bags
may be substituted.

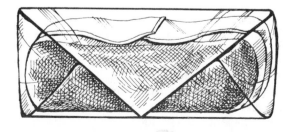

CURRIED TUNA SALAD

1 7-oz can tuna, or equal amount fresh cooked tuna
1 7-oz can crushed pineapple
1/2 cup plain yogurt or mayonnaise
1/4 cup flaked coconut
1/4 cup raisins
1 t curry powder
1 4-oz package alfalfa sprouts
4 large oranges, peeled and sectioned
1/4 cup toasted sunflower seeds (optional)

Drain tuna and pineapple well. Mix together the yogurt, coconut, raisins and curry powder. Fold in tuna and pineapple. Line 4 salad plates with sprouts; arrange orange sections in circle around sprouts. Spoon tuna mixture into center. Sprinkle each salad with 1 T of the toasted sunflower seeds.

Serves 4.

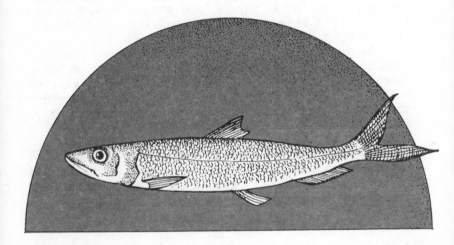

TUNA'S COMPETITION: PILCHARD

At this writing, there is a resurgence of a once-popular canned fish called pilchard. Found in the Pacific Ocean, this fish is a relative of sardines and herring. It is very similar to tuna in taste, and it is half the price of most canned tuna. Since the texture is somewhat softer, however, it would not substitute well for albacore, or where large chunks of tuna are desired. Try it in your next tuna salad, sandwich or favorite recipe. Your family may be pleasantly surprised!

Weakfish

If you have avoided this fish due to its uncomplimentary name, you have been missing a high-quality taste. A relative of striped bass, corvina, croaker and drum, the weakfish, also known as seatrout, is guilty only of having a weak mouth. Many frustrated fishermen have lost a prize when their hooks failed to hold in the delicate mouth tissue. Weakfish also has fragile flesh which needs icing immediately after catching to preserve its quality. Some cooks even advise freezing weakfish for a few days to firm the flesh and improve the texture. Be sure to check with your fish market first to see that the fish has not already been frozen; it should not be refrozen.

The sweet, lean and finely textured meat of this fish lends itself to a variety of cooking methods. Take care when turning it, however, as the fish breaks easily. Weakfish is well-complemented by herbs and herbed butters. It may also be substituted for sea bass, striped bass, and croaker, and vice versa.

In the market, you are most likely to find weakfish whole from 1 to 6 pounds, pan-dressed, or filleted from larger fish. Weakfish are moderately priced and seem most abundant during the warmer months.

Best cooking methods: baked, broiled, poached, pan fried.

SAUTEED WEAKFISH AMANDINE

2 lbs weakfish fillets, cut into serving-size pieces
Salt and ground pepper
1/2 cup milk
1/2 cup flour
1/2 cup butter
2 3-oz packages blanched, sliced almonds
Lemon wedges

Rinse and dry fillets and season with salt and pepper. Dip into milk and dredge lightly in flour. Saute in a large skillet in butter, turning once, until brown and tender, allowing 10 minutes per inch of thickness at the thickest part. Remove fish carefully to warmed platter and saute almonds in same pan, adding more butter if needed, until nuts are brown. Serve almonds over fillets; garnish with lemon wedges.
Serves 4-6.

WEAKFISH WITH TARRAGON

2 lbs weakfish fillets or 2 whole fish, about 1 1/2 lbs each,
    pan-dressed
1/2 cup milk
3/4 cup flour
Butter
1/4 cup minced fresh parsley
1-1 1/2 t dried tarragon or 1 T chopped fresh tarragon
1/2 cup dry white wine or vermouth
2 cloves garlic, pressed (optional)
Fresh whole tomato, peeled and chunked (optional)

Rinse and dry fish, brush with milk and lightly dredge in flour. In a skillet, saute fish in butter over moderate heat, allowing 10 minutes per inch of thickness at thickest part, until browned and tender when tested. Remove to a heated platter. Add the herbs to the butter in pan and stir to mix; add wine and simmer for 1 minute over low heat. Pour sauce over fish. For a variation, add garlic and tomato to simmering wine sauce, cook an additional minute until tomato is soft and serve over fish.
Serves 4-6.

Whiting

Whiting, also known as silver hake, is another member of the cod family and one of the most utilized species of fish. Besides its large direct consumption, whiting is processed into fish meal and oil and included in many animal food products.

Whiting has a tender, lean and soft-textured flesh with a delicate flavor. The fish are marketed whole (averaging 1 to 4 pounds), dressed and filleted. Since whiting is so abundant, the price is low, especially during the warmer months. Whiting can be substituted in most cod and haddock recipes, and vice versa.

Best cooking methods: baked, broiled, fried, poached.

CRACKER-COATED WHITING

2 lbs whiting fillets, rinsed, dried and cut into 2-in. pieces
3/4 cup flour
1/2 t salt
Freshly ground pepper
3/4 cup milk
2 cups cracker crumbs
Oil for deep frying
Tartar sauce
Lemon wedges

Dip fish pieces into flour mixed with salt and pepper, then into milk, then into cracker crumbs. For best results, allow coated fish to dry on waxed paper in refrigerator for 15-20 minutes. Fry at 370°F for 2 to 3 minutes, until golden. Drain on paper towels and serve with tartar sauce and lemon.
Serves 6.

MARINATED WHITING

2 lbs whiting fillets, cut into serving-size pieces
3 T each vinegar and lemon juice
1/3 cup vegetable oil
1 onion, thinly sliced
2 cloves garlic, minced
2 T chopped fresh parsley
1 bay leaf
Flour and ground pepper
Oil for frying
1 cup chopped, peeled tomatoes
Lemon wedges

Marinate fish for 1 hour in mixture of vinegar, lemon juice, oil, onion, garlic, parsley and bay leaf. Drain and fry fish; reserve marinade. Dredge fish in flour and pepper and pan fry in oil over high heat for 2 or 3 minutes per side. Remove fish carefully, drain on paper towels and place on heated platter.

To same pan, add chopped tomatoes and the reserved marinade; cook over moderate heat until slightly thickened, 5 or 6 minutes. Pour the tomato sauce over the fish and garnish with lemon wedges.
Serves 4-6.

Freshwater Fish

Catfish

People who haven't tried catfish probably can't appreciate that this fish has been a popular and plentiful food for thousands of years. Although there are two ocean species, the fresh-water family is the largest, with 28 varieties. Some of the best-liked are the channel, blue and white catfish.

Because the demand for catfish exceeds the supply, this fish is now being farmed in more than 30 states. Catfish is marketed fresh and frozen, either whole, skinned-dressed, filleted or steaked. Although oily, catfish has a tender, white and nutritious flesh.

Catfish should always be skinned before cooking; if you do it yourself, care should be taken to avoid the painful barbs found on the dorsal and pectoral fins. Skin the fish the way you would an eel. Make a circular cut through the skin just in back of the head. Continue around the head, behind each pectoral fin, and return to the original cut. Nail the catfish to a board by its lower lip, grab the skin with pliers and pull downward firmly. The skin should pull away in one piece. Remove the fish from the board, eviscerate it and cut off the head. Boning is not necessary, since catfish have only a spine which can be removed during filleting or after cooking the fish whole.

Best cooking methods: baked, broiled, grilled, smoked, sauteed, stuffed, deep fried.

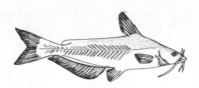

TRADITIONAL FRIED CATFISH

2 1/2 lbs catfish fillets, skinned and cut in half if large
Milk
1 1/2 cups finely ground white or yellow cornmeal
1 t salt
1 t ground pepper
1/2 t cayenne (optional)
Oil for deep frying
Seafood or tartar sauce

Wash and thoroughly dry fillets; place in a bowl with milk to cover and set aside. Mix cornmeal and seasonings together in a pie plate. One at a time, remove fillets from milk and coat evenly with cornmeal mixture. Arrange on wax paper and dry in refrigerator for 1 hour. Fry fish in oil at 375°F, a few at a time, about 3 minutes on a side, until brown. Drain well on paper towels, remove to a large platter and keep hot by placing in a 200°F oven. Serve with your favorite seafood sauce or tartar sauce.
Serves 6.

BARBECUED CATFISH

2 lbs catfish fillets
1 recipe Fresh Tomato Sauce, cooled, page 219
Lemon wedges

Marinate fillets in Tomato Sauce in refrigerator for 1 hour; turn fish once. Grill fish over moderate coals, about 3 minutes each side, basting often with sauce. A hinged wire grill works well as fish can be turned without breaking. Heat remaining sauce and serve with fish. Garnish with lemon wedges.
Serves 6.

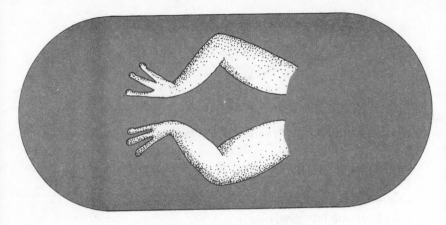

Frogs' Legs

If you can set aside visions of Kermit the Frog and your children's lovingly collected tadpoles, frogs' legs are a truly delicious adventure well worth trying. They are commercially raised in the United States and also in Japan, where they are a frozen and smaller product but, to most tastes, the superior one.

Frogs' legs have a delicate flavor and texture, similar to chicken. They require minimal cooking and are best when sauteed lightly with delicate herbs. Allow about 6 pairs of the small legs per serving, or more for hearty appetites.

Frogs' legs should be soaked in milk for 1 hour or more before cooking, to improve their flavor. The best method is to defrost frozen legs in milk overnight in the refrigerator, or for several hours at room temperature.

Best cooking methods: sauteed, pan fried, deep fried.

BASIC SAUTEED FROGS' LEGS

24 pairs fresh or thawed frogs' legs
4 cups milk plus 1 1/2 t salt
1 cup flour mixed with 1/2 t pepper, for dredging
Butter and cooking oil, equal parts, for sauteing
1/2 cup butter
4 cloves garlic, minced
3 T fresh lemon juice
1/2 cup chopped fresh parsley
Sauce Variations, page 131

If frozen, thaw frogs' legs in milk until thawed. If fresh, soak in milk 1 hour. Remove legs and shake off excess milk. Dredge in mixture of flour and pepper. Saute 4 to 6 legs at a time quickly in hot butter and oil. A nonstick pan works best since the legs tend to stick. Cook about 3 minutes on each side until delicately browned. As the legs are cooked, place them on a platter in a 200°F oven.

When they have all been cooked, melt 1/2 cup butter in the same pan and add the garlic. Cook just long enough to soften garlic, then add the lemon juice. Pour over the frogs' legs and sprinkle them with parsley. Also see sauce variations below.

Serves 4.

VARIATIONS FOR BASIC SAUTEED FROGS' LEGS

Frogs' Legs Sauteed with Herbs

For 4 servings, mix 1 cup toasted buttered fresh bread crumbs with 2 T chopped fresh parsley, 1 T dried chives and 1/2 t dried tarragon. When all frogs' legs are cooked, return them to the skillet and add the herb/crumb mixture. Toss gently to mix and serve with lemon wedges.

Frogs' Legs Sauteed with Onion and Mushrooms

For 4 servings, finely chop 1 small onion and 4 large mushrooms. When frogs' legs are all cooked, remove to heated platter and keep warm. Add 1/4 cup butter to the skillet and quickly saute onion and mushrooms. Return frogs' legs to skillet and toss gently to coat. Serve with chopped parsley.

Frogs' Legs Sauteed with Tomatoes and Garlic

For 4 servings, prepare Basic Frogs' Legs as far as removing them to a platter in a 200°F oven. Do not discard the pan juices from cooking the legs. To the cooking pan, add 4 cloves minced garlic and 4 peeled, seeded and chopped fresh tomatoes. Cook over medium heat for 5 minutes, stirring frequently. Place each serving of frogs' legs on heated plates, sprinkle with 3 T fresh lemon juice and 1/2 cup chopped fresh parsley and spoon the tomato sauce over each portion.

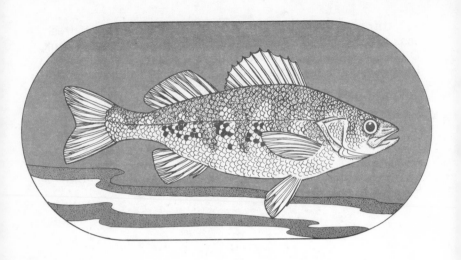

Perch

Of the 19 species of perch, the two best known commercially are yellow perch and walleye. Yellow perch is an important food fish to both commercial and sportsfishermen. Most abundant in the Great Lakes region, this perch is caught primarily in winter and is available frozen all year. At the market, it is available whole from 1/2 to 1 pound and filleted, with the firm white flesh virtually boneless.

Walleye, a close cousin to yellow perch and an equally important game fish, is an excellent food fish with a sweet white flesh. It is a true perch, unrelated to pike, although it is often marketed as yellow pike. Walleye is commercially important to the Great Lakes and parts of Canada, where these fish are gill-netted. Walleye comes to market whole, dressed, pan-dressed and filleted. It is also available frozen in one-pound blocks. It is a very versatile fish adaptable to all methods of cooking and can be served hot or cold.

Best cooking methods: baked, broiled, deep fried, sauteed, poached, planked (see Whitefish, page 141).

YELLOW PERCH IN BROWN BUTTER

6 whole perch, or 2 lbs fillets
Flour, salt and ground pepper
Butter
Brown Butter, or other Hot Butter variation, page 214
Lemon wedges

If using whole fish, clean and dress; if fish are small, split or leave whole. If using fillets, rinse and dry well. Dredge fish in flour to which salt and pepper have been added. Saute in hot butter, allowing 10 minutes per inch of thickness at thickest part, whether using whole fish or fillets. Remove cooked fish to hot platter. Prepare Brown Butter or other hot butter variation and serve over fish. Garnish with lemon wedges.
Serves 6.

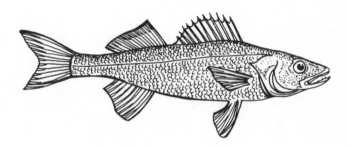

POACHED WALLEYE WITH ORANGE HOLLANDAISE

4 whole dressed walleye (yellow pike), about 1 lb each
Milk broth, see Simple Poaching Broths, page 206
Cheesecloth
Orange Hollandaise, page 211

Wrap fish in cheesecloth and poach in milk broth (see Poaching, page 22) until fish is tender, allowing about 10 minutes per inch of thickness at thickest part. Carefully lift fish from liquid and allow to drain on a rack for several minutes to firm up flesh. Unwrap and arrange on heated platter. Serve with Orange Hollandaise.
Serves 6-8.

BROILED PERCH

2 lbs perch fillets
1/2 cup pineapple juice
2 T vegetable oil
1 T lemon or lime juice
1 T brown sugar
1 T Worcestershire sauce
1/4 t salt

Rinse and dry fillets; set aside. Combine remaining ingredients and mix well. Marinate fillets in pineapple juice mixture for 1 hour. Lift fillets from marinade, place on greased broiler pan and brush with reserved marinade. Heat remaining marinade and keep warm. Broil fillets 4 inches from heat, allowing 10 minutes per inch of thickness at thickest part. It is not necessary to turn thin fillets as they tend to break. Baste often with marinade and test frequently for doneness. Serve remaining marinade with fish.

Serves 6.

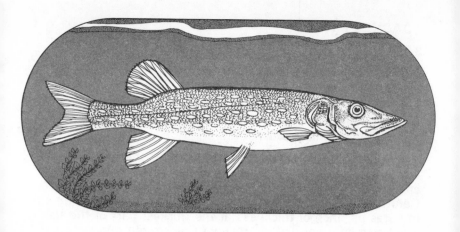

Pike

The vision that comes to most people's minds when they think of pike is not one of a succulent poached fish in a butter and herb sauce. If you have only had pan fried pike, you have missed a treat. Pike has a sweet white flesh that is firmly flaked and takes well to poaching, baking and smoking.

The three best-known members of the pike family are muskellunge, the largest, which weighs from 10 to 30 pounds; northern pike, which weighs from 4 to 10 pounds; and pickerel, which weighs up to 3 pounds. Although these are bony fish, the larger the fillet (from a fish weighing more than 4 pounds), the less the problem posed by the bones.

Pike is available year round, in areas where it is fished, as fresh whole dressed fish and fillets, and frozen blocks of fillets and steaks.

To properly dress and prepare pike, the slippery substance coating its body should first be removed. Scald the fish by pouring boiling water over it; the substance will congeal and can be easily removed.

Best cooking methods: poached, baked, smoked, pan fried. Pike takes well to all types of sauces, but should not be overpowered.

POACHED PIKE

1 whole dressed pike, 3-4 lbs, or 3-4-lb chunk
Court Bouillon, page 205
Cheesecloth
1/2 cup butter
1 T lemon juice
1/2 t dried rosemary, crushed

Prepare Court Bouillon, bring to boil, then simmer 1/2 hour before adding fish. Clean and prepare pike, wrap in cheesecloth (see Poaching, page 22) and lower into bouillon. Return to boil, reduce heat and simmer, covered, allowing 10 minutes per inch of thickness at the thickest part of the fish. Place fish on a hot platter, remove cheesecloth and keep fish warm. Melt butter and add lemon juice and rosemary. Serve hot over fish.

Serves 6-8.

PIKE KIEV

2 lbs pike fillets, cut into 6 portions
1/4 cup butter, softened
1/4 cup chopped green onions
1/4 cup chopped fresh parsley
1 T dried dill weed
1/2 t salt
1/4 cup cornstarch
2 eggs, beaten until foamy
1 1/2 cups dry bread crumbs
1/2 cup sesame seeds
Equal parts butter and oil, for sauteing
Lemon or lime wedges

With a thin, sharp knife, make a pocket in each portion of fish, as you would a pork chop. Cream butter with green onions, parsley, dill weed and salt; divide mixture equally among fish portions and spread in pockets. Dredge the fish in cornstarch; dip into egg, then into bread crumbs mixed with sesame seeds. Allow to dry in the refrigerator for 1/2 hour.

Heat equal parts of butter and oil in a large, heavy skillet and cook fish over medium heat, allowing 10 minutes per inch of thickness at thickest part, turning once. Fish is done when it flakes easily when tested at the thickest part. Serve with lemon or lime wedges.

Serves 6.

BAKED PIKE WITH HERBED CREAM SAUCE

1 whole dressed pike, 5-6 lbs
6 T butter, softened
1 clove garlic, pressed or minced
Salt
1 T minced fresh parsley
Pinch each of dried marjoram, summer savory and thyme
1/4 cup oil or melted butter, for basting
1 cup dry white wine or dry vermouth
2 T flour mixed with 2 T soft butter
1-2 t lemon juice
Salt to taste

Spread soft butter, to which pressed garlic has been added, inside cavity of fish. Sprinkle cavity with salt, parsley and dried herbs; close fish with string and skewers. Place fish in a large baking pan lined with two well-oiled sheets of heavy aluminum foil. Brush fish with melted butter or oil. Bake, uncovered, at 350°F for 10 to 12 minutes per inch of thickness at thickest part of fish. Baste every 5 to 10 minutes with white wine; check for doneness after 25 minutes. When cooked, transfer fish, still in foil, to a heated platter, allowing juices to drain off foil into baking pan. Strain pan juices into a small saucepan and place over low heat. Add the flour/butter mixture to saucepan and bring to a boil. Reduce heat and cook until thickened; season with lemon juice and salt to taste. When ready to serve, remove foil from fish; spoon a little sauce over fish and pass the rest.
Serves 6.

Trout

There are numerous species of trout, of which every angler has his favorite. The most familiar are brook, brown, lake and rainbow. The color, flavor and texture of each species is different due to environment, diet and size of fish. For those of us who don't fish the lakes and streams, trout is available fresh from trout farms. It is also marketed frozen, gutted, boneless and sometimes breaded. Flash-frozen hatchery trout can be better than fresh fish which has been held on ice for long periods.

Generally speaking, small trout from 6 to 10 inches is best cooked quickly, by deep frying or pan frying. Trout from 12 to 14 inches is best baked, broiled, poached or sauteed. Larger trout, 20 inches and up, is delicious stuffed and baked, steaked and broiled, smoked or poached. Larger trout can also be substituted in recipes calling for salmon. Larger trout needs no scaling and if prepared whole is easily boned after cooking.

Best cooking methods: fried, baked, broiled, poached, sauteed, smoked.

CAMPFIRE BREAKFAST TROUT

6 pan-dressed trout, 8-12 in.
1/2 lb bacon
Flour or cornmeal
Salt to taste
Campfire toast or muffins, heated in foil in the fire

Cook bacon in large skillet over campfire; drain on paper towels and reserve bacon fat in pan. Dredge fish in flour or cornmeal and saute in bacon fat, a few minutes on each side. Salt to taste after cooking depending on saltiness of bacon. Serve fish with bacon and warm campfire toast or muffins.
Serves 6.

HOT OR COLD POACHED TROUT

6 pan-dressed trout, 10-14 in.
Court Bouillon, page 205
1/2 cup butter melted with 1 T lemon juice and 1 T minced fresh parsley (for hot fish)
Cold mayonnaise, see page 216 for variations (for cold fish)

Simmer Court Bouillon for 1/2 hour, strain, return liquid to same pot or poacher and bring back to boiling. Add trout to pot and return liquid to boiling. Remove pot from heat, cover and let stand for 15 to 20 minutes, until fish is cooked. Carefully remove fish from pot and drain. Serve hot with melted butter, lemon juice and parsley, or serve cold with any cold mayonnaise variation.
Serves 6.
Note: For a dramatic presentation, use freshly caught trout. The protective film on unhandled fish, when it is dipped in vinegar, causes the fish to turn blue. To achieve this result, use tongs. Dip the fish into a combination of 2 parts boiling water mixed with 1 part vinegar until the skin turns blue. It is important to touch fish only with tongs or wet hands, to keep the protective film intact. When blue, transfer fish to boiling Court Bouillon and cook as above.

GRILLED BUTTERFLIED TROUT

4 trout, 10-14 in., cleaned and butterflied (Have your
    fishmonger show you or see illustration, page 31.)
1 1/2 cups Italian salad dressing, bottled or homemade
1/2 cup butter, melted
Lemon wedges

Marinate butterflied trout in salad dressing in a covered
dish for 30 minutes. Drain fish and cook on grill, skin side
down, for 8 to 10 minutes or until flesh turns white and flakes
easily. Do not turn. When cooked, serve with melted butter and
lemon wedges.
   Serves 4.

BAKED STUFFED TROUT IN FOIL

1 large trout, 4-6 lbs, cleaned, rinsed and dried, prepared for
    stuffing, see page 25
1/2 cup chopped celery
1/2 cup chopped onion
1/2 cup chopped mushrooms
1/3 cup butter
2 cups fresh bread crumbs
2 T dry white wine
Fish stock (see page 194) or water
Salt and pepper to taste
Melted butter
Lemon wedges

Saute celery, onion and mushrooms in butter until soft.
Stir mixture into bread crumbs in a bowl and toss well. Add
wine and fish stock or water, just enough to moisten. Season
with salt and pepper. Sprinkle cavity of fish with salt and pepper and fill loosely with stuffing. Sew or skewer fish closed and
place on thick, oiled aluminum foil. Remove head of fish if your
baking pan cannot accommodate whole fish. Brush fish well
with melted butter and add more wine if desired. Wrap fish
securely enough so that no steam can escape; place in baking
pan. Bake at 375°F, allowing 15 minutes per pound, turning
fish halfway through cooking. Check for doneness by testing at
the thickest part. When fish is done, loosen aluminum foil and
fold around fish; place on heated serving platter and garnish
with lemon wedges. Serve with more melted butter if desired.
   Serves 6-8.

Whitefish

Having spent summers in northern Michigan since childhood, I have always had fond memories of whitefish. Little did I know that many Maine lakes have an abundance of these wonderful fish which are eagerly sought after by fly fishermen every spring.

There are several species of whitefish found in North America. The smallest, known as cisco or chub, is marketed from less than 1 pound to 2 pounds. It is available fresh in areas where caught, otherwise it is marketed smoked. Lake whitefish is the most valuable commercial species from lakes in northern United States and parts of Canada. It is available fresh and smoked, and the usual market size is about 4 pounds. Round whitefish or menominee is found in the northern United States and is abundant in larger lakes in Maine where sportsfishermen account for most of the catch. The average size of this fish is from 1 to 3 pounds; it poaches and smokes well.

All these fish are considered moderately fatty and have a tender white flesh which takes well to poaching, baking, grilling, broiling and smoking. In northern Michigan, planked whitefish is the New England counterpart of clam chowder.

Best cooking methods: baked, broiled, grilled, poached.

SMOKED WHITEFISH APPETIZER SPREAD

1/2 lb smoked whitefish
Mayonnaise
Lemon juice
1 T finely minced onion
Party-size rye or pumpernickel bread rounds
Lemon wedges

Flake and bone whitefish; toss with enough mayonnaise to moisten. Add a squeeze of lemon juice and the onion; mix thoroughly and refrigerate for 1 hour. Serve in bowl surrounded with bread rounds and lemon wedges for garnish.

Makes about 1 cup.

GRILLED WHITEFISH

1 small whitefish, 1-2 lbs, or 1 large fillet, skin on
1/2 cup coarse salt dissolved in 2 cups water
Vegetable oil
1/2 cup butter, melted
1 T lemon juice
1 T fresh parsley

If whitefish is whole, split and bone it, leaving tail on but removing head. Completely immerse split fish or fillet in salt solution, then place fish on an oiled, hinged grill without shaking excess salt solution from fish.

Brush fish with a little of the melted butter, fasten grill and cook over moderate coals for 8 to 10 minutes per side, depending on thickness of fish. If fish becomes dry, baste with a little melted butter to which lemon juice has been added. Fish should have a nicely browned crust. Serve with remaining melted butter and lemon juice. Garnish with fresh parsley.

Serves 4.

PLANKED WHITEFISH

1 whole whitefish, 3-4 lbs, cleaned and gutted, split and boned, head on or off
Vegetable oil
Softened butter
Salt and pepper
Paprika
2 cups mashed potatoes with a beaten egg yolk added
Dried hardwood plank (preferably oak), large enough to hold split fish
Lemon wedges

Oil plank and place in a cold oven; heat to 400°F. Remove from oven, arrange fish on plank, skin side down, and dot with butter. Season with salt and pepper and bake for 10 minutes per inch of thickness at the thickest part. When almost done, border the plank around the fish with potatoes, using a pastry tube. Sprinkle fish lightly with paprika. Return to oven and bake until fish is done and potatoes are lightly browned. The fish can be served directly from the plank. Garnish with lemon wedges.
Serves 6-8.

Shellfish

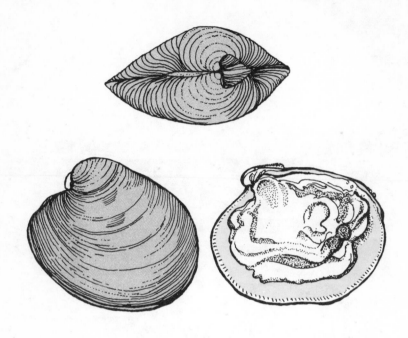

Clams

The clam family offers us a variety of edibles in varied shapes and sizes. On the Atlantic coast, the utilized species are the quahog or hard-shell clam, the soft-shell clam and the surf or bar clam.

Hard-shell clams are marketed according to size: the smallest or Little Neck is 3 to 4 years old, the Cherrystone is about 5 years old and chowder clam is the catch-all category for clams too large to be served on the half-shell. Small hard-shell clams are good steamed, on the half-shell, baked, broiled or fried. Large hard-shell clams (more than 3 inches across) are used in chowders and fritters and are baked-stuffed.

Soft-shell clams are usually marketed from 2 to 3 inches in length. These sweet clams are delicious steamed, deep fried or chopped and used in fritters or chowder. Because of the shell construction and their sandy or muddy habitat, soft-shell clams require cleaning and purging before they are eaten.

Surf or bar clams are very large, growing to 8 inches in some areas along the North Atlantic coast. More people are discovering that this popular ''cod bait'' is excellent when the foot is ground for use in chowders or fritters, and that the adductor muscles which hold the shells closed are much like scallops and can be prepared as such.

You will find clams at the market live in the shell, shucked and canned. They are sold by the dozen when in shells, and sometimes by the pound (steamers). Be sure to discard any clam that does not close when tapped on the shell, or has a badly broken or crushed shell. When stored at 40°F, live clams should keep for several days. Shucked clams are sold in their own juice in pint or quart containers. They can be refrigerated for a week, or frozen for 3 to 4 months. Do not refreeze clams that have already been frozen. Canned clams come chopped or minced in brine or clam juice, whole, smoked and in oil.

To freeze shucked clams, drain over a bowl of water and rinse meats in a brine of 4 t of salt to 1 gallon of water. Remove any shell bits or grit, drain and pack in small freezer containers. Cover with reserved clam liquor, adding a weak brine of 1 t of salt to 1 cup of water, if necessary. Leave 1/2 inch of headroom, seal tightly and label. Freeze at 0°F and store at that temperature for up to 4 months.

To purge clams, scrub them well under running cold water, place them in a large pot and cover them with lightly salted water — 4 t of salt to each gallon of water. Add 2 to 3 T of vinegar, which acts as an irritant and causes the clams to flush out their sand. Allow them to sit, undisturbed, for 15 to 30 minutes; drain and refrigerate or cook as you like.

Generally speaking, allow 6 to 12 hard-shell clams on the half-shell per person, 1 to 3 dozen steamed clams per person, and 1 pint to 1 quart fried clams per person.

Best cooking methods: baked, fried, steamed.

HOW TO SHUCK CLAMS

1 Hold clam firmly with hinged part of shell toward palm.
2 Use flat-bladed clam knife and insert blade between shells.
3 Carefully cut around muscles to loosen clam from top and bottom of shell.

DAVID'S HERBED STEAMED CLAMS

8 doz steamers or 6 doz Cherrystones, scrubbed and purged
1/2 cup water
1/2 cup dry white wine or dry vermouth
2 cloves garlic, mashed
1 medium onion, cut into chunks
1/2 t salt
2 T butter
6 whole peppercorns
1/4 t dried tarragon
Melted butter

Combine all ingredients except clams and melted butter in a kettle, sized so clams, when added later, would fill pot 2/3 full. Bring liquid to a boil and simmer for 5 minutes. Add clams. Steam until they open, 6 to 10 minutes (hard-shell clams take longer). Discard any clams that don't open. Strain broth into cups and serve with clams and melted butter.
Serves 4.

STEAMED CLAMS

1-2 doz clams per person, hard-or soft-shell, scrubbed and
purged
Lightly salted water, or sea water
Melted butter
Lemon wedges

Place clams in a large kettle with 1/2 in. lightly salted water or sea water. Do not use badly broken or cracked clams. Place on high heat and steam just until shells open, 5 to 10 minutes (hard-shell clams take longer). Discard any clams that do not open. To each person serve a bowl of clams, a cup of the strained broth for dipping and a dish of melted butter to which a squeeze of lemon juice has been added. Have extra bowls on hand for empty shells.

Soft-shell Clam

PASTA WITH CLAMS

2 doz small Cherrystones, well scrubbed
1/4 cup olive oil
3 cloves garlic, minced or pressed
1 small green pepper, seeded and chopped
1/2 cup chopped fresh parsley
1 2 lb, 3 oz can chopped or ground tomatoes
1 t dried basil
Dash cayenne
Salt to taste
1 lb small tubular pasta (rigatoni)
Boiling water
1 lb large shrimp, raw/fresh or frozen, peeled and deveined
3 T butter

Heat oil and saute garlic, green pepper and parsley; don't let brown. Add tomatoes, basil, cayenne and salt; simmer for 5 minutes. Set aside.

Cook the pasta in boiling water for 10 minutes, stirring often. At the same time, add clams in shells and shrimp to tomato sauce and simmer for 10 minutes. Drain pasta and run under cool water, then add to clam mixture. Add butter and transfer to covered casserole dish; bake at 350°F for 20 minutes.

Serves 6.

Note: You may replace shrimp with any cooked fish or shellfish to suit your taste, such as mussels, whitefish, lobster or crab. If using cooked seafood, add just before baking.

CLAMS CASINO

2 doz Cherrystones on the half-shell
4 slices uncooked bacon, chopped
3 T minced onion
3 T minced green pepper
2 T lemon juice

Saute bacon until partly cooked, then add onion and green pepper. Cook until soft but not browned. Place clams on a broiler pan, sprinkle them with lemon juice, then top with vegetable/bacon mixture, about 1 t of topping per clam. Broil until hot, about 5 minutes.

Serves 4-6.

MUSHROOMS WITH CLAM STUFFING

7 oz minced clams, canned or fresh, drained; reserve juice
2 doz medium-size fresh mushrooms
1 clove garlic, minced
Butter
1/2 cup cracker crumbs
1/4 cup grated Parmesan cheese
4 T butter, melted
1 t minced parsley
1/2 t Worcestershire sauce
Lemon juice

Clean mushrooms, remove and chop stems and saute stems with garlic in a little butter. Add remaining ingredients, except lemon juice, and mix well, adding only enough clam juice to hold mixture together. Set aside.

Quickly saute mushroom caps in butter, then stuff caps with clam mixture. Bake at 350°F for 15 minutes and serve hot. Squeeze a few drops of lemon juice on each mushroom if desired.

Makes 24 appetizers.

BAKED CLAMS OREGANO

2 doz Cherrystones on the half-shell
3 cloves garlic, pressed or finely minced
2 T minced fresh parsley
1 t dried oregano
3/4 cup fresh bread crumbs
Olive oil
Lemon wedges

Place clams in shallow baking pan. Thoroughly mix the garlic, herbs and bread crumbs and add just enough oil to moisten mixture. Top each clam equally with mixture, about 1 T, and bake at 400°F for 8 to 10 minutes. Serve with lemon wedges.

Serves 4-6.

Note: This recipe can be varied by adding 1/4 cup grated Parmesan cheese to 1/2 cup bread crumbs and moistening crumbs with melted butter instead of olive oil.

BAKED STUFFED CLAMS

18 hard-shell clams (Cherrystones or small chowder clams)
1/2 large onion, chopped
1/2 cup butter
2/3 cup flour
2 cups milk, warmed
1/2 cup clam liquid, reserved from cooking clams
2 T chopped parsley
Dash cayenne pepper
Dash nutmeg
1 1/2 cups fresh bread crumbs
2 T butter, melted
Cocktail Sauce, page 217, or lemon wedges

Cook clams in 1/2 inch of water until they open, 8 to 10 minutes. Cool, remove meats from shells and reserve 1/2 cup broth and 24 shells. Chop clam meats and set aside.

Saute onion in butter until soft, stir in flour and cook until bubbling. Remove pan from heat, stir in warmed milk and return to heat. Cook until thickened and bubbling. Add clam liquid, clams and seasonings. Stir well and remove from heat; let cool, then refrigerate to ease handling.

Scrub 24 clam shells and fill with chilled mixture. Toss bread crumbs with melted butter and sprinkle on top of clams. Bake at 375°F for 10 to 15 minutes, then broil lightly to brown. Good served with Cocktail Sauce or lemon wedges.

Serves 6; makes 24.

FRIED CLAMS IN CRUMBS

1 qt shucked clams, soft- or hard-shell
Flour
1 cup milk
2 cups cracker or fine dry bread crumbs
Oil, for deep frying
Tartar Sauce (see page 216), or your favorite seafood sauce

Drain excess liquid from clams. Roll in flour, dip in milk and roll in crumbs. Place on a cookie sheet lined with waxed paper and dry in refrigerator at least 10 minutes. When all clams have dried, cook a few at a time, so they aren't crowded, in hot oil, 375°-380°F, for about 30 seconds, or until golden brown. Drain on paper towels and serve hot with Tartar Sauce or your favorite seafood sauce.

Serves 4-6.

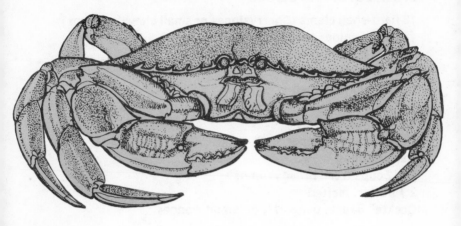

Crab

Crabs are an extremely valuable resource on both coasts of the United States. From the Pacific coast comes the king, snow and Dungeness crabs. Native to the Atlantic coast are the blue, red, rock and Jonah crabs. It isn't necessary to live along either coast to have access to this delicious shellfish, since canning and freezing make crabmeat available year round.

Crabmeat varies in taste, texture and color, and not all types of crabmeat are interchangeable. All are versatile enough, however, to be baked, fried, broiled and used in salads, soups, chowders, souffles and casseroles. Live crabs are delicious steamed or boiled and eaten with melted butter or your favorite seafood sauce.

King crab from Alaska is one of the largest of the species. It is marketed cooked — either frozen or canned. The legs and claws are usually sold whole, cooked and frozen, while the back meat is cooked and canned.

Snow crab, a spider crab smaller than the king crab, is sold in the same manner. It is also available at premium prices in frozen blocks of cut up leg meat. When buying this type of frozen crabmeat, be sure to check for signs of drying/freezer burn. The same applies to picked-frozen crabmeat. Not all crabmeat freezes well.

Dungeness crab, a member of the rock crab family, is marketed canned, or fresh and fresh-cooked in areas where it is fished.

Blue crabs are considered one of the most important shellfish in the United States. In their hard-shell form, they are available fresh-whole, cooked or canned, and their delicious meat comes in lumps, flakes or as claw meat. When blue crabs shed, they are called soft-shell and are very popular cooked and eaten whole, shell and all. Soft-shell crabs come live in the shell, cooked, canned and frozen.

The meat of red crabs is considered such a superior product that it is often substituted for king crab in recipes. It is available frozen in 6-ounce containers, live in the shell, cooked and canned.

Rock and stone crabs do not have a large commercial market but are harvested in small quantities and are available locally. Rock crabs and their cousins Jonah crabs are usually a sideline of fishermen, who sell them to lobster pounds or businesses set up to cook and pick the claws and bodies and sell this fresh, sweet crabmeat to local markets. Most often, only the claws of stone crabs are available. Fishermen who catch these crabs twist off the claws and throw the crabs back to regenerate new ones. The claws are cooked immediately and sold as is or frozen. They are shipped all over the country from Florida, where they are caught primarily, but they are still in short supply and remain quite expensive.

Live crabs should be selected just like lobsters; choose the liveliest ones and store them, out of water, in the refrigerator until you are ready to use them. Like lobsters, crabs will drown if they are kept in fresh or unaerated water.

When using canned, frozen or fresh crabmeat, remember that it has already been cooked and needs only to be heated through. Remember also to always check for shell fragments.

Best cooking methods: boiled, steamed, fried (soft-shell).

WHOLE BOILED CRABS

2 doz live hard-shell crabs, or 6 crabs per person
6 qts water, sea water if available
2 T salt for each quart <u>fresh</u> water
2-3 T Crab Boil seasonings, available at most seafood markets
  (optional, see Note)
1/2 cup lemon juice
Melted butter
Lemon wedges

Bring water, seasonings and lemon juice to a boil and boil for 10 minutes. Plunge the crabs into the pot and start timing when the crabs are all added and the water has returned to a boil. Cook for 15 to 20 minutes, depending on size of crabs, or allow about 8 minutes for each pound of crab. Drain crabs and allow to cool for 5 minutes. Serve whole, on a newspaper-covered table, with small knives, plenty of napkins and melted butter and lemon wedges if desired.

Serves 4.

Note: If Crab Boil is not available, you can substitute a mixture of the following: 1 T ground pepper, 2 t allspice, 20 whole cloves, 2 t thyme, 10 bay leaves (broken), 2 t celery seed, and 1 t dry mustard. (These amounts are for 6 quarts of water and 2 dozen crabs.) For plain boiled crabs, omit Crab Boil or the equivalent seasonings.

HOT CRABMEAT AND MUSHROOMS WITH BROWN RICE

12 oz crabmeat, fresh, canned or frozen
8 oz sliced mushrooms, fresh, or canned and drained
2 T chopped onion
1 T each minced parsley and chopped chives
1/4 cup butter
1/4 cup flour
1 cup milk, or mushroom liquid and milk to equal 1 cup
3 egg yolks, lightly beaten
2 cups sour cream
2 or 3 T sweet sherry
Hot buttered, brown rice

Saute mushrooms, onion, parsley and chives in butter until onion is soft. Blend in flour and cook until smooth and bubbling. Blend in milk and stir until thickened. Stir 1/4 cup hot sauce into egg yolks, then add egg yolk mixture to remaining sauce and stir constantly until thickened again. Add the crabmeat, sour cream and sherry; heat just until mixture begins to bubble. Serve at once over hot buttered brown rice.
Serves 6.

CRABMEAT SALAD

6 oz crabmeat, fresh, canned or frozen
1/2 cup mayonnaise
1/2 t dried mustard
1/2 t horseradish
2 T cocktail sauce, or more to taste
3 green onions, chopped
1/2 cup chopped celery
1 T minced parsley

Mix all ingredients and refrigerate 20 minutes to develop flavors. This mixture is delicious stuffed in avocado halves or scooped-out tomatoes, or in the center of a Tomato Aspic (page 120) or jellied cucumber salad mold.
Makes 1 1/2 cups.

HAWAIIAN CRAB AND FRUIT SALAD

1 lb king or snow crabmeat in lumps
1 small fresh pineapple or 1 16-oz can pineapple rings, drained
    and cut in half
Crisp salad greens
1 avocado, sliced and dipped in lemon juice
1 small cantaloupe or papaya, peeled, seeded and sliced
1 12-oz can mandarin oranges, drained
1 cup sour cream
1/2 cup mayonnaise
Juice and grated rind of 1 lime
1/3 cup chopped chutney
1 cup chopped macadamia nuts

Remove leaves and rind from fresh pineapple. Cut fruit into rings, then cut each ring in half. Cover a large serving platter with salad greens, then arrange fruit and crabmeat in rows: pineapple slices, avocado slices, crabmeat, cantaloupe or papaya slices, and mandarin oranges. Cover platter with clear plastic wrap and chill until ready to serve.

Mix sour cream with mayonnaise, lime juice, lime rind and chutney; place in small serving bowl. Chop macadamia nuts and place in another serving bowl. When ready to serve, remove plastic wrap from platter and serve with the bowls of dressing and chopped nuts to sprinkle on top.

Serves 6.

CRABMEAT CURRY

3 6-oz containers crabmeat, fresh, canned or frozen
1 onion, chopped
2 ribs celery, thinly sliced
1 firm, tart apple, peeled and chopped
1/2 cup sliced fresh mushrooms
2 T butter
1 T curry powder, or to taste
2 cups chicken broth or stock
3 T cornstarch mixed with 1/3 cup cold water
2 cups half and half cream
Salt to taste
Hot white or brown rice
Condiments

Saute onions, celery, apple and mushrooms in butter until onions are soft. Stir in curry powder and cook until lightly browned. Add chicken stock, let simmer a few minutes, then add water/cornstarch mixture and cook until thick. Add cream and heat, but do not boil. Add salt to taste, stir in crabmeat and simmer until heated through, stirring gently. Serve over white or brown rice with the following condiments in small dishes on the side: chopped salted peanuts, chopped hard-cooked eggs, raisins, chopped white or green onion, chutney, coconut (flaked or grated), chopped banana, chopped tomato, chopped cucumber, pine nuts, slivered almonds, chopped green pepper, crumbled bacon. Make up your own combinations!

Serves 6-8.

INDIVIDUAL CRABMEAT CREPE APPETIZERS

7 oz flaked crabmeat, fresh, canned or frozen
16 large dinner crepes (from your favorite recipe)
1 cup grated Swiss cheese
1/2 cup chopped water chestnuts
1/2 cup mayonnaise
1 T chopped green onion
1 t lemon juice
1/4 t curry powder
1/4 cup minced fresh parsley

Prepare crepes and cool. Cut three 2 1/2-in. circles from each crepe. Fit circles into greased 1 3/4-in. muffin tins. Pick over canned crab for pieces of shell, then combine crabmeat and all ingredients except parsley. Mix well and place a rounded teaspoon of filling in each cup. Bake at 400°F until heated, 10 to 12 minutes. Sprinkle each cup with minced parsley.

Makes 48 appetizers.

Lobster

There are three commercially important species of lobster on the domestic market: the American lobster, the spiny lobster and the lobsterette.

The American lobster was once so plentiful that it could be found in tidal pools and taken by hand, to be used for fertilizer or cod bait. The demand for these delicious crustaceans has now grown to such proportions that many biologists and fishermen feel that the lobster stock is declining. In Maine, where the industry began, the conservation measures are the strictest of all the lobstering states. Maine feels that these standards should be adopted by the other states to protect this valuable resource.

The average market size of the American lobster is from 1 to 5 pounds, although it has been known to grow to 45 pounds. At the market, lobster is classified according to size: chicken lobsters, 1 pound; quarters, 1 to less than 1 1/2 pounds; large, 1 1/2 to less than 2 1/2 pounds; and jumbo, more than 2 1/2 pounds.

The majority of lobster meat comes from the tail, then the claws and body. Generally speaking, a 1 1/2-pound lobster is an adequate portion for one person. When buying cooked lobster meat, allow about 1/3 pound per person. When buying cooked whole lobster in the shell, if you have doubts as to its freshness, pull the tail out straight and release it. If it snaps back to a curled position, the lobster was alive when cooked. This test works only on uncut lobsters.

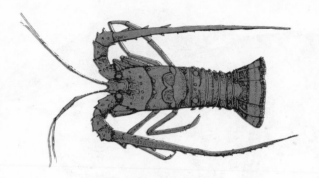

The spiny or rock lobster, as it's called at the market, is a clawless lobster found in tropical waters. It is most abundant in Florida, although frozen tails are imported from South Africa, Australia, Chile and New Zealand. The tail — the only edible portion of this lobster — has slightly coarser meat than that of the American lobster, but it is equally delicious. Depending on the size, allow one to two lobster tails per person. Commercially available rock lobster seldom weighs more than 5 pounds, although it has been known to reach 17 pounds.

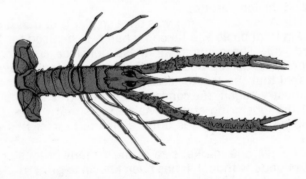

Lobsterette refers to the smaller members of the lobster family, more commonly marketed as Danish lobster tails and/or Dublin Bay prawns. Lobsterette is more delicate in taste and texture than the American lobster. Like the spiny lobster, the edible meat comes from the tail, which is about 4 inches long and is usually marketed frozen, except in Florida and parts of South America, where it is fished. These lobsters are quite expensive, when they can be found. Allow four small tails per person.

Best cooking methods: boiled, baked, stuffed/baked.

HOW TO COOK MAINE LOBSTERS

First, select the liveliest lobsters, allowing a 1 1/2-pound lobster per person. Some people prefer boiled lobsters; others prefer steamed. Whichever you choose, the times are as follows for a single lobster, even up to granddaddy size, if you should ever find one: 1 to 1 1/4 pounds, cook for 10 to 12 minutes; 1 1/2 to 2 pounds, 15 to 18 minutes; 2 1/2 to 5 pounds, 20 to 25 minutes; 6 to 10 pounds, 25 to 35 minutes; 10 to 15 pounds, 35 to 40 minutes; 15 to 20 pounds, 40 to 45 minutes; 20 to 25 pounds, 1 hour.

For a flavorful way to boil lobster, fill a large kettle two-thirds full of water and add a splash of vinegar, a bay leaf, a few whole peppercorns and 2 to 3 T minced parsley. If you prefer, use plain salted water — 2 t salt for each quart of fresh water — or sea water. Bring to a boil and plunge the lobsters into the water head first. Cover the pot and start timing when the water returns to a boil. Time according to the weight of one lobster, adding 1 minute more for each additional lobster. **Don't Overcook!**

If you steam your lobsters, use a large pot and place a rack in the bottom. Add to the pot 1 1/2 inches of water with 1 t of salt, or use sea water. Bring the water to a boil. To quiet the lobsters (They tend to thrash about.), hold them under warm tap water for just 1 minute; it makes them sleepy and less active. Then add them to the boiling water all at once, and cover. If you have to layer the lobsters to fit into an under-sized pot, place the larger ones on the bottom, since those closer to the water cook faster. Do not layer them more than two rows high. If you are cooking a large number of lobsters, cook a few at a time; the cooked ones will remain warm while you cook the next batch.

When the steam begins to rise again, start timing as for boiled lobsters. Let the cooked lobsters cool a bit to facilitate handling. Serve them with melted butter and plenty of napkins; it's messy if you do it thoroughly!

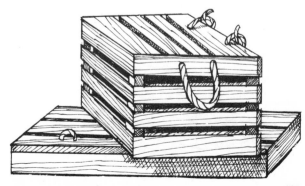

HOW TO EAT MAINE LOBSTER

The Neat Way. When the cooked lobster is cool enough to handle, turn it onto its stomach and, with a sharp knife, make a lengthwise cut towards the tail from the point where the tail and body are joined. Cut all the way through. Turn the lobster and cut through in the other direction, towards the head. Split the lobster and remove the sand vein from the tail and stomach (sand sac) and from the head. The green tomalley (liver) can be eaten or discarded, according to personal preference. Some find it is as delicious as the rest of the lobster. It is located in the body cavity and is easily recognizable by its color.

This is a good way to serve cold lobster for a buffet or luncheon, with mayonnaise, cocktail sauce or lemon wedges.

The Messy Way. When the cooked lobster has cooled slightly, twist the claws from the body, twist the tail from the body and serve everything with melted butter, lemon wedges and a set of lobster claw crackers and picks. To remove the meat from the tail, twist off the tail fin and squeeze the tail together at the sides until the underside cracks. With a fork, push the tail meat from the smaller end out through the wider opening, pull off the back strip of meat and remove the sand vein. If you like to pick the bodies, insert your thumb under the back edge of the body shell and pull the insides down. Remove the sand sac near the head and pick the rest; the meat is hiding where the legs meet the body. The green tomalley (liver) is also edible. You can suck the meat from the eight small legs as well.

When eating lobster this way, cover your table with old tablecloths or newspaper to keep clean-up at a minimum.

I find that the best dishes to serve with lobster are salads and vegetable casseroles that don't require using extra butter. We serve ratatouille, a casserole which includes tomato, zucchini, eggplant, green pepper and onion. This can be served hot or cold, and nicely complements the richness of the lobster.

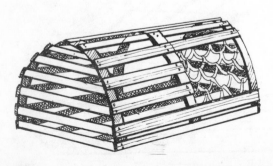

HOW TO COOK SPINY OR ROCK LOBSTER TAILS

Since you will most likely be dealing with the frozen product, let the tails defrost in the refrigerator. They will be more tender than those cooked frozen or partially thawed. Lobster tails can be steamed, boiled, deep fried or broiled. They should not be baked, since this method of cooking toughens them.

The shell of the tail is very strong and requires cutting prior to cooking. If you plan to boil the tail, cut out the undershell, leaving the rest intact. To broil, cut through the top part of the shell just to the tail fan, leaving the undershell uncut. Spread the top shell and meat apart and brush it with melted butter. This is the ''butterfly'' form.

To boil, heat enough water to boiling to cover the tails and add 1 T of vinegar for each quart of water. When the tails have all been added, cover the pot; when the water has returned to the second boil, start timing as follows: 4 ounces (including weight of shell), 5 minutes; 5 ounces, 6 minutes; 6 ounces, 7 minutes; 7 ounces, 8 minutes; 8 ounces, 9 minutes; 9 ounces, 10 minutes. When serving the smaller tails — the 4- or 5-ounce size — allow two tails per person.

When broiling the tails, butterfly each tail and broil them shell-side up, 4 inches from the heat for 5 minutes, regardless of size. Turn them flesh-side up, brush them with melted butter or basting sauce and broil as follows: 4 to 6 ounces, 6 minutes; 7 to 8 ounces, 7 minutes; 9 to 10 ounces, 8 minutes. To prevent the broiled tails from drying out, add a little water to the bottom of the broiling pan while cooking.

FREEZING LOBSTER MEAT

When we have extra cooked lobster meat or wish to take advantage of our summer catch, we freeze lobster meat to use in stew and quiches during the winter months. I freeze cut-up chunks in whole milk and include the thawed liquid along with the meat in cooked dishes. The milk seems to protect the meat from freezer burn and taste, and freezing toughens the texture only slightly. If you prefer, lobster meat can be packed in rigid meal-size freezer containers and frozen without liquid. With both methods, leave 1/2 inch of headroom for expansion.

ELEGANT STUFFED LOBSTER

6 lobsters, 1 1/2 lbs each, cooked and cooled
1 cup sliced fresh mushrooms
1 large red sweet pepper, seeded and chopped
1 medium onion, chopped
2 T cooking oil
6 oz crabmeat, fresh, frozen or canned
4 T butter
3 T flour
1 1/2 cups milk
3 T sweet or dry sherry
2 T grated cheddar or Swiss cheese
Salt and pepper to taste
1 cup dry bread crumbs mixed with 2 T melted butter
Melted butter

While lobsters are cooling, saute mushrooms, pepper and onion in oil until onion is soft, not brown. Add crabmeat and stir gently; remove from heat and set aside.

Make a cream sauce by melting butter in a saucepan, stirring in flour and cooking until bubbly. Remove from heat, stir in milk and return to low heat. When sauce begins to thicken and bubble, add sherry and cheese, cooking until cheese melts. Season with salt and pepper. Pour cream sauce into vegetable/crabmeat mixture and stir gently. Set aside.

With a pair of kitchen scissors, cut out undershell of each lobster tail and remove the tail meat from the shell. Remove back strip and clean away sand vein; then cut meat into small pieces and add to vegetable/crabmeat mixture. With scissors, cut through undersides of lobster bodies between small legs; spread bodies open. Remove stomach and drain excess water from cavity, leaving tomalley (liver) if desired. Leave claws on lobsters and wrap each claw in a piece of aluminum foil to cover. Heat the vegetable/seafood mixture until hot but not bubbling, and stuff each lobster with as much as bodies will hold. Sprinkle about 2 1/2 T of the buttered bread crumbs over the stuffing and bake at 350°F for 15 minutes, until crumbs are browned and stuffing bubbles a little. Serve with melted butter for the claw meat.

Serves 6.

DANISH LOBSTER TAILS IN CURRY SAUCE

3 doz Danish lobster tails, cooked according to package
    directions
2 T chopped onion or shallots
2 T butter
1 T curry powder
1 t A-1 sauce
1 1/2 cups Bechamel sauce, page 209
1/3 cup dry white wine
1 cup sour cream
1/2 t Kitchen Bouquet
Salt and ground pepper
Hot buttered rice
1 T minced fresh parsley

Remove cooked lobster tails from shells and set aside. Saute onion in butter until soft, then add curry powder and brown lightly. Add the next six ingredients and heat. Add lobster tails to sauce and stir to coat. When mixture is hot but not boiling, place tails onto the hot rice and cover with remaining sauce. Sprinkle parsley over all.

Serves 6.

Note: This dish is good served with any of the condiments that accompany curry dishes, such as chutney, raisins, coconut, etc. See the list on page 157 under Crabmeat Curry.

LOBSTER QUICHE A LA LEONARD

1 cup cooked lobster meat, cut into bize-size pieces (see Note)
2 T minced onion
3 T butter
1/2 t salt
Freshly ground pepper
2 T dry vermouth, or dry white wine
3 eggs
1 cup heavy cream
1 T tomato paste or cocktail sauce
1/4 t salt
1 8-in. pastry shell, precooked 5 minutes at 375°F
3/4 cup grated Swiss cheese

Saute onion in butter until soft. Add lobster and stir for 2 minutes over low heat. Add 1/4 t of the salt, pepper and wine; simmer 1 minute. Cool and set aside.

Beat eggs with cream, tomato paste and remaining 1/4 t of the salt. Add cooled lobster and pour mixture into pie shell. Sprinkle with cheese and bake at 375°F for 25 to 30 minutes.

Serves 6.

Note: Cooked crabmeat or shrimp can be substituted for lobster.

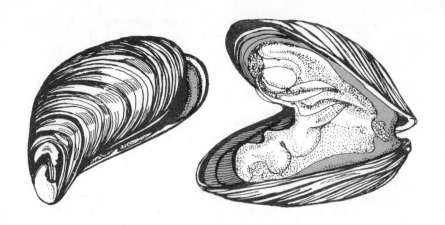

Mussels

Found in all the oceans of the world, mussels have been a favorite seafood of many cultures for hundreds of years. Unfortunately, mussels have long been overlooked by most American cooks. They are finally gaining acceptance and favorable publicity, however, and are now becoming popular in American kitchens.

The edible blue mussels, especially plentiful along the New England coast, contains high-quality protein, vitamins and minerals, and almost no fat. It is delicious by itself and in chowders, stews and dips. It can also be substituted in most clam and oyster recipes. It is marketed live in the shell, canned, packed in oil or tangy sauce, pickled and smoked.

When buying fresh mussels or gathering your own, take only those that are tightly closed or that close when tapped or gently squeezed. Mussels from the market have already been cleaned somewhat, so leave them undisturbed and refrigerated until ready to use. Mussels you gather should be rinsed in salt water, separated from rocks and empty shells and then refrigerated until ready to clean and use. To make certain you gather fresh mussels, take them from below the low tide mark. (They will be under water even at low tide.) You should know whether or not the area you are gathering from is contaminated or closed due to "red tide," a harmful organism stored in large quantities particularly by mussels. Since mussel beds are now closely monitored, notices are posted and news of any closing is broadcast frequently. The best seasons for gathering mussels are fall, winter and early spring; the danger of "red tide" is greatest during the summer.

To clean mussels, scrub them under running water and scrape off any barnacles with a dull, heavy knife. Cut off with scissors or pull out with your fingers the dark byssus threads or "beard" which protudes from the middle of the shell. If you pull towards the large, rounded end of the shell, the threads should pull out easily. If they don't, they can be removed after cooking.

After the mussels have been cooked, discard any that have not opened. Mussels are best when cooked within a day or two of gathering, unless you are close enough to the ocean to give them a good drink of sea water. If you steam them within 24 hours of gathering your own, you need not add any water. Just heat the pan over moderate heat. When the liquid starts escaping from the shells, turn up the heat and steam 5 or 6 minutes, until all the shells are opened and the meats have loosened from the shells. Never fill the pan more than two-thirds full of mussels, to allow room for the shells to open. If you need to add a liquid for cooking, allow 1/2 cup of water or wine for every 2 quarts of mussels.

When serving steamed mussels as a main course, allow about 2 dozen 2 1/2 to 3-inch long mussels per person. (Two dozen shucked mussels will yield about 1 cup of meat.)

To freeze mussels, shuck them as soon after gathering as possible and follow the directions for freezing clams on page 147. Small containers are best and take less time to thaw. Once the mussels have thawed, do not refreeze them.

If using canned mussels in chowders or dips, drain off the brine and substitute clam juice in the recipe.

Best cooking methods: steamed, fried, baked.

BROILED MUSSEL APPETIZERS

Good served with hot French bread to soak up the juices.

2-3 doz mussels on the half-shell
1/4 lb butter
1/2 cup minced fresh parsley
1/2 cup chopped onions
1-3 cloves garlic, minced
1/2 cup dry bread crumbs
Hot French bread

Cream butter with next four ingredients, by hand or in a food processor. Spread a little of the mixture over each mussel and refrigerate until ready to cook. Arrange mussels in a shallow baking pan and broil for 5 minutes in a preheated broiler until butter is bubbling and crumbs have browned. Serve with hot French bread.

Serves 4-6 as a first course.

MUSSELS ADRIATIC

4 doz mussels in the shell, scrubbed and debearded
2-3 cloves garlic, pressed or minced
1/4 cup butter
1/4 cup olive oil
4 T tomato paste
3/4 cup water
1/4 cup dry white wine or dry vermouth
Hot Italian bread or hot cooked rice

In a pot large enough to accommodate mussels without being more than 2/3 full, gently cook garlic in butter and oil. Add next 3 ingredients and simmer, covered, for 10 minutes. Add mussels and cook, covered, 8 to 10 minutes. When all mussels have opened, spoon into soup dishes and pour sauce over each. Serve with hot Italian bread, or serve over rice for a heartier meal.

Serves 4-6.

FRIED MUSSELS

1 quart shucked mussel meats
Recipe for Fried Clams, page 151
Tartar Sauce, page 216

Prepare mussels as for Fried Clams. Serve with Tartar Sauce or your favorite cocktail sauce.
Serves 4-6.

GREEN MUSSELS

3 doz mussels, steamed just until opened, top shell removed
Cayenne, or black pepper
1 package of frozen spinach souffle, thawed
6 slices crisply cooked bacon, crumbled

Place mussels in the half-shell in a shallow baking pan. Carefully sprinkle a dash of cayenne or black pepper on each mussel. Place 1 t of the spinach souffle on top of each mussel; top with crumbled bacon, 1 piece for every 6 mussels. Broil 5 minutes, 3 to 4 inches from heat.
Makes 36 appetizers or 6 first-course servings.

HERBED STEAMED MUSSELS

6 doz mussels in the shell, scrubbed and debearded
Recipe for David's Herbed Steamed Clams, page 148

Follow recipe for David's Herbed Steamed Clams, allowing 5 to 7 minutes for cooking. Discard any mussels that do not open.
Serves 4-6.

MOULES SUSANNE

3 doz mussels in the shell, scrubbed and debearded
1 lb spaghetti
1/2 cup olive oil
4 cloves garlic, minced
1 medium-size zucchini, scrubbed and cut into small pieces
2 medium-size fresh tomatoes, cut into small wedges
1/4 cup minced fresh parsley
Salt and ground pepper to taste
1 cup dry white wine

Cook spaghetti according to directions on package; drain and keep warm.

In the oil, saute garlic until soft. Reduce heat, add zucchini and cook until almost tender; add tomatoes, parsley, salt and pepper. While the sauce is cooking, steam the mussels in wine in a pot large enough to accommodate them all without being more than 2/3 full. Cook until all shells are wide open, 5 to 7 minutes, depending on size. Drain mussels and keep warm.

When ready to serve, add the mussels (in their shells) and sauteed vegetables to the spaghetti; toss to coat and evenly distribute shells and sauce. This is best served immediately while all ingredients are piping hot. Serve with cold, dry white wine. Very special!

Serves 8.

Oysters

People who love oysters aren't just fanciers, they are addicts! For them, a mere six oysters on the half-shell won't do; in fact the record is 350 oysters consumed at one sitting by one person. It has also been noted that in one year 1 1/2 billion pounds of oysters were consumed worldwide.

In the United States, we are familiar with the three species of oysters native to our waters. The Eastern oyster accounts for the largest oyster harvest. It can be found the length of the Atlantic coast and into the Gulf of Mexico. Its shape, taste and texture change as its environment changes, and it may be called blue point, Cape Cod, Kent Island or a number of other regional names. The two species native to the Pacific coast are the Western or Olympia oyster and the Pacific oyster, which has its origins in Japan. The Olympia is considered the quality oyster, although it is not very abundant at this time. The Pacific is larger, meatier and not, to my tastes, as good as its eastern relative. Many restaurants on the West coast depend on daily shipments of the Eastern oysters.

At the market, you will find oysters fresh in the shell; fresh shucked; shucked and frozen; smoked and canned in oil; fresh-canned in brine; and canned in soups, stews and bisques. When selecting fresh oysters in the shell, check to see how recently they arrived and from where, and check to make sure the shells are tightly closed. Northern oysters are best in fall and winter; Gulf coast oysters are best in winter and spring. When buying containers of shucked meats, buy only those that are in clear liquid, not milky looking juices. Fresh shucked oysters have very little odor and, if properly packed in ice (shucked and in containers), they should keep in the refrigerator for several days.

Shucking your own oysters comes easier with practice. Use a blunt, heavy, rounded knife; if it slips, your fingers will thank you. Placing the hinge part of the shell in your palm, push the blade between the shells near the hinge and twist until the shells pop open. Run the knife around the shell until you cut the adductor muscle that holds the oyster together. Shuck the oysters over a bowl with a strainer to catch the natural juices and prevent bits of shell from falling into the bowl. See Oyster Knife Method diagram, page 176.

When serving oysters on the half-shell, first make sure they are well chilled, then check opened oysters for bits of shell around the edges. Loosen the meat gently and leave it in half the shell; do not drain the juices. Serve them on a bed of ice. Allow 6 to 12 oysters per person.

I have encountered one serving exception which is actually a matter of taste. The European or Belon oyster is a small, delicate morsel which is becoming more popular in this country due to successful aquaculture, especially in Maine. These oysters were served to me at room temperature with a lemon wedge. They were every bit as good as the chilled version.

When baking oysters in the half-shell, it helps to bake them on top of coarse rock salt. This balances the shells and keeps them hot at the table.

If you must freeze oysters, use raw oysters as fresh from the water as possible. Shuck them yourself if possible. Freeze as for clams (see page 147), or try freezing individual oysters in ice cube trays, covering them with oyster liquor or weak brine. When frozen, pop out the cubes and store them in freezer bags. This way, you can thaw as many or as few as you need.

Thawed oysters should be used only for cooked dishes. One pint will make about six servings in casserole dishes, but you may need to allow more if you are serving them fried. Use frozen oysters within two months of freezing.

Purists eat oysters "as is," without sauce. For those who prefer a hot cocktail sauce, there are several good brands on the market, or make your own with this combination:

HOT COCKTAIL SAUCE

2 t prepared horseradish
4 T chili sauce or ketchup
2 t vinegar
2 T lemon juice
Dash Worcestershire and Tabasco sauces
Salt to taste

————— ►•●•◄ —————

Best cooking methods: baked, broiled, roasted.

OYSTERS FLORENTINE

1 pint fresh, shucked oysters, well drained
2 packages frozen chopped spinach, thawed
1 1/2 cups Bechamel sauce, page 209
1/2 cup dry white wine or dry vermouth
1/2 cup chopped green onion
1/2 cup sliced mushrooms, sauteed in butter
Salt and freshly ground pepper to taste
1 cup grated sharp cheddar cheese

Press thawed spinach through a sieve to remove extra juice. Set aside. To Bechamel sauce, add wine, onions and sauteed mushrooms; season with salt and pepper. Set aside.

In a separate bowl, mix just enough sauce with spinach to moisten; spread spinach in the bottom of a shallow, greased 2-quart baking dish. Top with the oysters and cover with sauce. Sprinkle grated cheese over all and bake at 350°F for 30 minutes or until hot and bubbling.

Serves 6.

BAKED OYSTERS ON THE HALF-SHELL

2 doz fresh oysters on the half-shell
4 8-9-in. cake pans each filled with 1/2 in. rock salt
One of the following toppping recipes:

1) **1/2 cup chili or cocktail sauce**
   1/2 cup grated Parmesan cheese
   2 slices bacon, partly cooked and each cut into
   12 pieces

   Place 1 spoonful of sauce on each oyster; top with grated cheese and 1 piece of bacon. Bake at 450°F until bacon is cooked and oysters begin to curl at edges, 4 to 5 minutes.

2) **1/2 minced onion**
   2 T minced green pepper
   Butter
   1/2 cup chili or cocktail sauce
   2 slices bacon, as above

   Saute vegetables in butter and mix with chili sauce. Spoon over oysters and top with bacon. Bake as above.

3) **1/2 cup dry bread crumbs**
   1/4 cup grated Parmesan cheese
   1/4 cup minced fresh parsley
   2 T chives
   1/2 cup butter, softened

   Cream all ingredients together and place 1 spoonful of mixture on each oyster. Bake at 475°F for 4 to 5 minutes, until topping is golden and oysters start to curl at the edges.

Each recipe serves 4 as a first course.

OYSTER STUFFING

1 pint fresh shucked oysters, drained; reserve liquor
1 medium onion, chopped
2 stalks celery, chopped
6 T butter
8 slices stale bread, cubed into 1/2-in. pieces
1/2 t dried thyme
1/4 t dried sage
2 T lemon juice
Salt and freshly ground pepper

Saute onion and celery in butter until soft, about 5 minutes. Add bread cubes and saute until browned, about 7 minutes. Remove from heat and add herbs and oysters that have been sprinkled with lemon juice. Fold in gently, adding some of the reserved oyster liquor for a more moist stuffing. Season to taste with salt and pepper.

Makes 4 cups.

Note: This amount of stuffing will fill a 5-6-pound chicken or a 6-pound fish. Double the recipe for an 11-pound turkey. You can also bake stuffing in a greased 1-quart casserole dish at 350°F for 25 minutes.

CAN OPENER METHOD

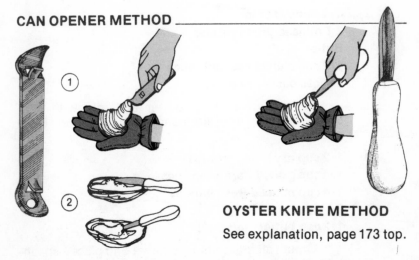

OYSTER KNIFE METHOD
See explanation, page 173 top.

1 Insert pointed end of opener into hinged part of shell.
2 Push and pry open; then use ordinary knife to cut adductor muscles and loosen meat.

Periwinkles

People who have never been introduced to periwinkles wouldn't know them from common snails. These little creatures are delicious; however, you just can't eat them in a hurry.

There are two edible types of periwinkle along the East Coast from Canada to the Gulf of Mexico. The "northern" periwinkle is usually gray to olive in color with brown or red bands. The "southern" or marsh periwinkle, which seems to be heading farther north each year, is yellow with brown spots.

Periwinkle shells are usually not larger than 1 inch across and are squat and conical in shape. They can be found all along the water's edge, usually on seaweed, rocks and pilings. When gathering "winkles," make sure each shell has a live occupant. Take only shells that are stuck to something; that way, you can see if the periwinkle withdraws into its shell when disturbed.

The meat of this creature has a nutty flavor and can be eaten boiled with melted butter or baked with garlic butter. Since they are so small, gather a lot; 6 dozen will serve about four people.

Periwinkles can be kept for a day or two in the refrigerator in the shell; if held longer, check them for any dead ones. To prevent them from crawling all over your refrigerator, cover them; they waste no time in making their getaway!

When cooking "winkles," boil or steam them just until the hard lid or operculum falls open. The meats should then come out easily with the point of a medium-size safety pin. They are wound into their shells like springs, so unwind them as you pick them out. Make sure you remove the operculum; it is not edible. The "winkles" can be eaten right away with melted butter, or cooked, refrigerated and used in other recipes.

Best cooking methods: baked, broiled, stuffed.

BAKED WINKLES

6 doz periwinkles, cooked and picked
1/2 cup butter, softened
1/4 cup minced fresh parsley
2 T minced green onion
2 cloves garlic, minced
Salt to taste
24 large snail shells or clam shells, or 4 small custard cups
Hot French bread, sliced

Cream butter with remaining ingredients, except winkles and shells. Dry winkle meats thoroughly with paper towels, and mix them with the garlic butter; let stand 2 hours. Then stuff snail shells with the mixture, or divide mixture among the clam shells or custard cups. Bake at 450°F for 10 minutes, until butter begins to bubble and brown. Serve with hot sliced French bread. The winkle meats and butter are delicious spooned onto the bread. I think you'll be pleasantly surprised!

Serves 4.

Scallops

Scallops have been considered an important seafood worldwide for centuries. The shells have inspired artists and served as religious symbols.

Although there are several hundred scallop species, only a few are of commerical importance to the East Coast of the United States. The sea scallop is the most abundant; it is fished primarily from deep waters off the Maine coast, but has been found as far south as New Jersey. The large shells measure up to 5 inches across and the scallop muscle can be 1 1/2 inches across. The bay scallop is considered by many gourmets to be the prime scallop, although I find the sea scallop equally delicious. Both can be used interchangeably in all scallop recipes.

Nowhere near as abundant as the sea scallop, the small, sweet bay scallop is found nestled in the eel grass in protected coves and bays. Several species can be found along the eastern and Gulf coast from Cape Cod to Florida. Their shells average about 3 inches across.

Because scallops are unable to stay tightly closed when out of water, they quickly lose body moisture and die. They are usually shucked on board fishing ships and iced immediately. If you gather your own scallops, shuck and chill them as soon as possible to maintain quality.

Scallops are probably the easiest of all bivalves to shuck, since they continually open and close, allowing you quick entry with a blunt knife to sever the muscle. The orange-colored coral or roe is considered a delicacy and can be cooked like any roe. (See page 87 under Shad.)

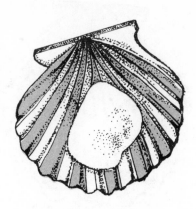

When buying fresh scallops, look for smooth, plump meats that are slippery looking but not slimy. Scallops packed in containers should be almost free of liquid and have a fresh odor. They are best when used the same day, but may be held for up to 2 days if the container is iced.

Some commercial distributors "soak" scallops in fresh water to increase their size. The meat of such scallops has lost flavor and quality; it appears white instead of pinkish and the edges are rough textured and white in places.

Fresh scallops can be eaten raw, pickled, poached, baked, broiled, fried, sauteed; used in stews and chowders; or served chilled with spicy sauces. Because they are so delicate, scallops require only minimal cooking — about 5 minutes to poach, 6 minutes to saute or 10 minutes to broil. Large scallops can be quartered or sliced across the grain in two or three wafers to make them go farther and cook more evenly. When frying or sauteing, make sure that the scallops are dry and that the pan is hot before adding butter or oil, to prevent burning and sticking. Allow about 2 pounds of scallops for six people.

To freeze fresh scallops, use the freshest available. Pack them tightly in freezer containers and cover them with a little brine (1 t of salt to 1 cup of water), leaving 1/2 inch of headroom for expansion. You can also place the scallops in plastic freezer bags, gently working all the air out, then twisting the bags shut. This method assures that there will be nothing in with the meats but their own natural juices. Frozen scallops stored at 0°F or less can be held for 3 to 4 months. They can be used in any recipe, but are not good eaten raw after thawing.

Best cooking methods: baked, broiled, sauteed, deep fried, pan fried, poached.

POLYNESIAN SCALLOPS

1 lb scallops, cut in half if small or in quarters if large, rinsed
    and dried well
1/4 cup flour
1 egg, beaten
1 1/2 cups grated coconut, finely chopped in blender or
    processor
3/4 cup chutney, chopped
1/4 cup butter
Oil, for deep frying

Cut scallops in half (or in quarters if using large sea scallops). Dredge in flour, dip in beaten egg, then roll in coconut.
Let dry on waxed paper in refrigerator for 10 to 15 minutes.

While scallops are drying, heat chutney and butter in a
saucepan and cook over low heat until butter is melted and
mixture is thoroughly heated. Keep warm.

In a deep skillet, heat 2 inches of oil to 375°F and fry the
scallops, a few at a time, until coconut is browned lightly, about
1 1/2 minutes. Drain on paper towels and keep warm until all
are done. Serve on wooden toothpicks with warm chutney
sauce.

Makes 2-4 dozen appetizers.

SAUTEED SCALLOPS WITH GARLIC AND TOMATOES

1 1/2 lbs scallops, cut in half if small or in quarters if large,
    rinsed and dried well
Flour
3 T butter and 3 T oil
3 cloves garlic, minced
Salt and freshly ground pepper
1 large tomato, cut into small chunks
1/2 cup minced fresh parsley
Lemon wedges

Roll scallops in flour. In a skillet, heat oil and butter and
cook scallops 3 to 5 minutes over moderate heat, tossing to coat
while cooking. Add garlic and mix well, shaking pan to turn
scallops; add salt and pepper. Add tomatoes and cook briefly
until soft, then add parsley and toss scallops to coat. Serve with
lemon wedges.

Serves 4.

SCALLOPS FRIED IN ALMOND COATING

1 lb scallops, cut in half if small or in quarters if large, rinsed
    and dried well
1/4 cup soft bread crumbs
1/4 cup blanched almonds
1/2 cup flour
1/4 t salt
Freshly ground pepper
1 egg, beaten
2 T milk
Oil for frying
Tartar Sauce, page 216 or Cocktail Sauce, page 217

Place bread crumbs and almonds in a blender and process
at high speed until mixture is finely crumbed. Place in shallow
bowl and set aside.

Combine flour, salt and pepper in another shallow bowl,
and egg and milk in a third bowl. Roll scallops in flour, dip in
egg and roll in crumbs. Place on waxed paper and dry in refrigerator for 10 minutes. Fry in hot oil at 375°F for 1 to 2 minutes,
until golden. Do not crowd scallops in fryer. Drain and serve
hot with Cocktail or Tartar Sauce.

Serves 4.

SCALLOPS IN HONEY AND BUTTER

2 lbs scallops, cut in half if small or in quarters if large, rinsed
    and dried well
1 cup dry bread or cracker crumbs
1/4 lb butter melted with 3 T honey
1/4 cup vegetable oil

Roll scallops in crumbs and divide them equally among 6
individual greased baking dishes or ramekins. Combine honey
butter and oil, and drizzle evenly over each portion of scallops.
Bake at 475°F for 10 to 15 minutes.

Serves 6.

COQUILLES SAINT-JACQUES WITH CRABMEAT

1 lb scallops, cut in half if small or in quarters if large, rinsed
    and drained
3/4 cup dry white wine or dry vermouth
1/4 cup water
1 T butter
1 T minced fresh parsley
1 small onion, sliced
1 small bay leaf, broken
2 t lemon juice
1/4 t salt
1/4 cup butter
1/4 cup flour
1 cup light cream
2 T grated Swiss or Parmesan cheese
Ground pepper and salt to taste
Dash nutmeg
1/4 cup chopped mushrooms, canned or fresh, sauteed in
    butter
6 or 7 oz fresh crabmeat
Hot cooked rice (optional)

Combine first 9 ingredients, except scallops, in a medium skillet over high heat. Reduce heat, add scallops and simmer, covered, 2-3 minutes. Strain, reserve liquid and keep scallops warm and covered.

In a 1-quart saucepan, melt butter, add flour and cook until bubbly. Add cream and 1 cup of scallop liquid; stir constantly until thickened and bubbling. Add cheese, salt and pepper, nutmeg and mushrooms; stir until cheese melts. Add crabmeat and scallops and cook over low heat until mixture is hot; adjust seasonings. Serve over rice or place in 6 ramekins and broil for 4 minutes until flecked with brown.

Serves 6.

Shrimp

Shrimp is by far the most popular seafood in the United States. It is an excellent source of protein, vitamins and minerals; it is easily digestible; and it is low in calories.

Many species of shrimp are found off the East Coast. They vary in size as well as color, but are all similar in taste and texture, except for small Maine shrimp which have a sweeter taste and a more delicate texture.

At the market, you will find shrimp presented in a variety of ways: raw with or without heads; fresh and frozen with and without shells; cooked and breaded/frozen; and canned. Rely on your senses of touch and smell to determine the freshness of raw shrimp. It should have a briny, ocean smell and should feel firm whether shelled or not. A strong iodine odor and/or flavor, which can be the result of diet, doesn't indicate spoilage; however, some people find it offensive.

I prefer to buy raw shrimp in their shells and cook them that way. They are easier to peel when cooked and the shrimp seem more tender and juicy than those bought already peeled. In addition, I find that frozen cooked shrimp are not as tender or tasty than those I cook myself.

Uncooked shrimp are classified according to size: tiny, up to 160 per pound; small (Maine), 31 to 35 per pound; medium, 25 to 30 per pound; large, 16 to 20 per pound; jumbo, 10 to 15 per pound; colossal, fewer than 10 per pound. To allow for loss of volume in peeling, buy about 2 pounds of raw shrimp in the shell for 1 pound of cooked, peeled meat. Allow 2 to 2 1/2 pounds of raw shrimp for six servings.

The sand vein which runs along the back of the shrimp can be removed before or after cooking, depending on the recipe. I find it unnecessary to devein Maine shrimp since the veins are so small.

Because shrimp are so versatile, they can be cooked in any number of ways. They are delicious hot or cold and in simple or rich sauces.

Best cooking methods: sauteed, baked, boiled, broiled, fried, stuffed.

BOILED SPICED SHRIMP IN BEER

2 lbs raw shrimp in shells
1 12-oz can beer
2 cups water
1 clove garlic, minced
1 1/2 t salt
1/2 t dried thyme
2 bay leaves
1 t celery seed
1 T minced parsley
Dash cayenne pepper
2 T lemon juice
1 shot bourbon (optional)
Melted butter

Rinse shrimp but do not peel. Combine remaining ingredients except melted butter and bring to a boil; simmer, uncovered, for 5 minutes. Add shrimp and return to boil. When shrimp begin to float to the top, about 30 seconds for very small shrimp and about 3 minutes for large shrimp, cover pan and remove from heat. Let stand 20 minutes to allow shrimp to absorb flavors. Drain and serve with melted butter; guests peel the shrimp themselves.

Serves 6.
Note: Shrimp cooked this way are excellent in cold dishes. Just cool, peel and use as desired.

SCAMPI (Shrimp in Garlic Butter)

2 lbs large raw shrimp in shells
1/4 lb butter
1/4 cup vegetable or olive oil
2 cloves garlic, minced
1 T parsley flakes or 2 T minced fresh parsley
3/4 dried basil
1/2 t dried oregano
1/2 t salt
1 T lemon juice

Peel and devein shrimp, leaving tails attached. Butterfly the shrimp by cutting down the inside lengthwise, taking care not to cut through the shrimp. Spread open and arrange in a shallow jellyroll pan with tails pointing upward. Mix butter, oil, seasonings and lemon juice and pour over shrimp. Bake for 5 minutes at 450°F, then broil another 5 minutes, until shrimp becomes flecked with brown. Spoon a little of the pan juices/garlic butter over each serving.
Serves 6.

SHRIMP CURRY

1 1/2-2 lbs small raw shrimp in shells, or 1 lb cooked shrimp
    meat
Curry sauce from Crabmeat Curry, page 157
Boiling water, seasoned with salt, lemon slice and onion slice
Hot cooked rice
Condiments from Crabmeat Curry, page 157

Make curry sauce and keep warm. Rinse and peel raw shrimp and simmer a few minutes in enough seasoned boiling water to cover. Remove from heat and drain. If large shrimp are used, remove sand vein after cooking. Add cooked shrimp to curry sauce and heat through. Serve with rice and condiments.
Serves 6-8.

STIR-FRIED SHRIMP WITH ASPARAGUS

1 lb small raw shrimp, peeled and deveined
1 lb fresh asparagus, washed and trimmed of tough stem ends
1 t grated fresh ginger root
1 T dry or sweet sherry
1 T soy sauce
1 T cornstarch
1 clove garlic, minced
4 T vegetable oil
1/4 cup chicken broth or water
3 green onions, chopped
1 t sugar
Dash cayenne (optional)
Cooked white or brown rice

Slice asparagus diagonally into pieces 1/4 in. thick. Set aside. In a glass bowl, combine ginger root, sherry, soy sauce, cornstarch and garlic; stir until cornstarch is well mixed in, then add shrimp and toss well to coat. Let stand 10 minutes or longer in refrigerator.

Heat 2 T of the oil in a wok or large skillet and add asparagus; toss well to coat with oil and stir fry about 1 minute. Add chicken broth, cover pan and simmer for 30 seconds. Uncover and cook 1 minute more, then remove asparagus and liquid to a bowl and keep warm.

In same pan, heat remaining 2 T oil. Drain shrimp (reserve marinade) and stir fry until the shrimp turn color, about 1 minute. Add the cooked asparagus with liquid and reserved shrimp marinade. Heat through, adding green onions, sugar and cayenne. Stir well and serve over rice.

Serves 4.

Note: If you wish to substitute larger shrimp, cut them in half lengthwise and again crosswise. Broccoli flowerets, cut up, can be substituted for asparagus.

SUPER SHRIMP PIZZAS

2 lbs small raw shrimp in shells, or 1 lb cooked shrimp meat
Salted water
1/3 cup chopped onion
3 or 4 cloves garlic, minced
1/2 cup salad oil
3 6-oz cans tomato paste
1 1/2 t dried oregano
1/3 cup minced fresh parsley
3 unbaked 9-in. pizza crusts
1 lb grated Mozzarella cheese

Rinse raw shrimp and simmer in salted water for 1 or 2 minutes until just cooked. Drain well, cool, peel and set aside.

Saute onion and garlic in oil until tender but not browned. Add tomato paste and simmer about 5 minutes. Remove from heat and add oregano and parsley. Place pizza crusts on greased cookie sheets and on each crust spread 1/3 of tomato mixture, arrange 1/3 of the shrimp, then cover with 1/3 of the cheese. Bake in a hot oven, 425°F, for 20 minutes, or until crust is browned and cheese is melted. Cut each pie into slices and serve.

Serves 6.

PICKLED SHRIMP

3 lbs medium raw shrimp in shells
1 cup salad oil
3/4 cup chopped onions
3 cloves garlic, minced
2 t salt
1/4 t ground pepper
3/4 cup cider vinegar
1/2 t dry mustard
1/2 t dried tarragon
Dash cayenne
1 medium onion, thinly sliced

Rinse, peel and dry shrimp. Heat 1/2 cup of the oil in a skillet and saute onions and garlic for 3 minutes; do not brown. Add shrimp, 1 t of the salt, and pepper, and cook 3 minutes more. Set aside.

While shrimp are cooling, combine remaining 1/2 cup of oil, 1 t of the salt, vinegar, mustard, tarragon and cayenne. In a large glass bowl, layer shrimp and sliced onions and pour marinade over all. Cover and refrigerate at least 24 hours.

Serves 12-16 as an appetizer.

GOLDEN FRIED SHRIMP

1 1/2 lbs large shrimp, peeled and deveined, tail sections left on
2 eggs, beaten
1/2 t salt
1/2 cup flour
1/2 cup dry bread crumbs or cornmeal
Oil for deep frying
Tartar Sauce, page 216 or Cocktail Sauce, page 217
Lemon wedges

When deveining shrimp, cut lengthwise through back, just enough to butterfly but not cut through. Dip each shrimp in egg mixed with salt, then in flour which has been mixed with crumbs or cornmeal. Place coated shrimp on waxed paper in refrigerator to dry for at least 15 minutes.

When ready to cook, heat oil to 375°F and fry shrimp a few at a time, 2 minutes or more, depending on size of shrimp. Drain on paper towels. Serve with Tartar Sauce or Cocktail Sauce, and lemon wedges.

Serves 4-6.

OVEN FRIED CURRIED SHRIMP WITH
HOT MARMALADE SOY DIP

2 lbs medium raw shrimp in shells
1 cup dry bread crumbs
1 t curry powder
1/2 t salt
Dash ground pepper
1 egg, beaten with 1 T water
2 T butter, melted
2 T vegetable oil
Hot Marmalade Soy Dip (recipe follows)

Peel shrimp, devein, rinse and drain. Set aside. Combine bread crumbs, curry powder, salt and pepper in shallow pan. Dip shrimp in egg and water mixture, then roll in crumbs to coat well. Place on a well-greased baking sheet and drizzle butter mixed with oil over each shrimp. Bake at 500°F about 10 minutes or until golden brown. Serve with Hot Marmalade Soy Dip.

Serves 6-8.

HOT MARMALADE SOY DIP

1/3 cup orange marmalade
1/4 cup lemon juice
1/4 cup soy sauce
1 clove garlic, minced
Dash powdered ginger
1 t cornstarch

Combine all ingredients in a small saucepan and mix well. Cook over medium heat until mixture begins to bubble, then reduce heat and cook, stirring constantly, until mixture is clear and thickened. Serve hot with shrimp.

Makes 3/4 cup.

SIMPLE SHRIMP CANAPES

1 lb tiny cooked shrimp, canned or frozen and thawed
Party rye bread or small slices French bread
Butter
Lettuce
Mayonnaise
Lemon wedges

Drain shrimp well and pick over for bits of shell. Lightly toast bread; spread sparingly with butter. Add a piece of lettuce, about 1 T of shrimp and a dollop of mayonnaise. Garnish with a small lemon wedge. The number of servings depends on the number of shrimp per bread slice and the size of the bread slices. A simple but delicious appetizer.

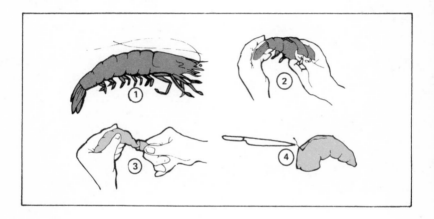

TO PEEL RAW SHRIMP

1. Twist body away from tail section.   2. Peel away shell and legs.   3. Remove tail shell by gently squeezing.   4. Remove sand vein with sharp knife by making a slit all the way down the back and lifting vein out.

Chowders, Soups and Stews

The best seafood soups start off with a good fish stock; plain water just doesn't do justice to the rest of the ingredients. The trick to having the right stock when you need it is to make a large pot of stock and freeze it for future use. It is really worth the extra effort!

Lean fish are generally better in chowders than oily fish, and firm-fleshed fish are better than soft-fleshed, which tend to fall apart. Do not boil the chowder after the fish or milk/cream has been added; the fish will become tough and the milk or cream may separate.

FISH STOCK

2 lbs fish heads and assorted bony trimmings
Water
1 carrot, sliced
1 rib celery, quartered
1 onion, sliced
2 T minced parsley
6 whole peppercorns
1/2 bay leaf
2 or 3 slices of lemon
1 cup dry white wine or dry vermouth

Place all ingredients in a large pot with 2 quarts of water or more to cover. Bring to a boil and skim off any foam, then reduce to simmer and cook for 1/2 hour, uncovered. Cool stock, then strain through a fine mesh strainer or several layers of cheesecloth. Stock will keep in the refrigerator for 3 days and in the freezer between 4 and 6 months. Freeze in 2-cup containers for faster thawing.

Makes about 2 quarts.

BASIC CHOWDER BASE

1 qt fish stock, page 194, or boiling water
3 large potatoes, peeled and cut into 1/2-in. chunks
2 medium onions, coarsely chopped
1 bay leaf
1/2 t thyme
3 T butter
3 T flour
3 cups light cream, or milk and cream combined, warmed
Salt and ground pepper to taste
2 T minced parsley
2 T dry white wine or dry vermouth (optional)
2 oz salt pork, diced and fried until crisp (optional)

Bring the stock or water to a boil in a large pot and add potatoes, onions, bay leaf and thyme; reduce heat and simmer until potatoes are just done. If you are adding uncooked fish or seafood (see Note), add to the stock and simmer until fish or seafood is cooked.

For a thick chowder, melt the butter in a small saucepan and stir in flour. Cook over low heat until mixture bubbles, then add 1 cup of the hot fish stock and stir until blended and thickened slightly. Pour this mixture back into the large pot and stir gently over moderate heat until stock has thickened. If you are using cooked fish or shellfish, add to the thickened stock now and cook over low heat until fish is hot. When you are ready to serve the chowder, add warmed cream, salt and pepper, parsley and wine and heat thoroughly but do not allow to boil. Garnish with salt pork.

Serves 6.

Note: Amounts of fish or shellfish to add: 2 lbs firm white-fleshed fish fillets; **or** 1 cup cooked, minced clams or mussels, fresh or canned; **or** 1 lb raw or cooked shrimp, peeled and deveined, cut up if large; **or** 1 lb raw or cooked scallops, cut up if very large; **or** 1 1/2 cups fresh or frozen cooked crab or lobster meat.

BOURRIDE (French Fish Stew)
WITH AIOLI SAUCE (Garlic Mayonnaise)

2 lbs assorted fish fillets, such as bass, haddock, flounder or
    halibut
1 large onion, coarsely chopped
2 cloves garlic, minced
2 small bay leaves, broken
2 strips orange rind
1/4 t fennel seeds, crushed
1 t salt
Freshly ground pepper
1 cup dry white wine or dry vermouth
2 T salad oil
6 cups water
2 egg yolks
Aioli Sauce, at room temperature (recipe follows)
6 slices toasted French bread, 1 in. thick, baked at 350°F for
    4 minutes each side and then rubbed with a cut clove of
    garlic

Rinse fish in cold water, dry, cut into 2-in. pieces and set aside.

In a large, heavy pot, combine the next 10 ingredients and bring to a boil. Reduce heat and simmer, covered, for 10 minutes. Strain broth and return to same pot. Bring broth back to a boil, add fish pieces, reduce heat and simmer, covered, until fish flakes when tested. Carefully remove fish from broth to a warm serving dish, cover and keep warm in a 175°F oven. Strain and reserve 2 cups of the broth and keep warm.

In a medium-size bowl, beat 1 cup of the Aioli Sauce with the 2 egg yolks until mixed, then gradually add 1 cup of the warm broth, stirring constantly, until blended. Add remaining cup of broth to a saucepan, stir in egg yolk/broth mixture and heat slowly, until the sauce begins to thicken. Remove from heat and cover to keep warm.

To serve, place 1 slice of toast in the bottom of each of 6 large, warm soup bowls. Pour a little sauce over the toast, place pieces of poached fish on top and pour a little more sauce over the fish. Pass the remaining cup of Aioli Sauce.

Serves 6.

AIOLI SAUCE

3 large cloves garlic, finely minced
2 large egg yolks, at room temperature
1/2 t dry mustard
1/2 t salt, or more to taste
Dash cayenne pepper
2 cups salad oil, at room temperature
1 1/2 T white wine vinegar
1 T lemon juice

In a blender container or mixing bowl, beat together the first 5 ingredients until well mixed. Continue beating/blending and add oil, a few drops at a time, then in a slow, steady stream until all the oil is added and the mixture is thickened. Blend in the vinegar and lemon juice and adjust salt to taste. If the mixture should curdle (from adding the oil too fast), beat another egg yolk in a clean bowl and add the curdled mixture slowly, stirring constantly. This will restore the sauce to a smooth consistency. Serve at room temperature with Bourride.

Makes 2 cups.

BAHAMIAN FISH CHOWDER

3 lbs red snapper or any firm, white-fleshed fish, skinned, filleted and cut into 2-in. chunks

3/4 cup lime juice

Salt and pepper

1/3 cup butter

1 large onion, chopped

1 green or red sweet pepper, seeded and chopped

1/2 cup chopped celery

4 cups canned ground tomatoes or cut-up fresh tomatoes

1 6-oz can tomato paste

4 large potatoes, peeled and cubed

1 large carrot, chopped

Few drops Tabasco

Marinate fish chunks in 1/2 cup of the lime juice, salt and pepper; refrigerate 1/2 hour. Drain fish and pat dry with paper towels. Saute in butter over medium high heat until lightly browned. Remove fish and reserve.

To the same pan, add onion, green pepper and celery, saute until just beginning to brown. Add tomatoes, tomato paste, potatoes and carrot; simmer 1 hour. Add fish and simmer another 10 to 15 minutes, until fish flakes and is tender. When ready to serve, add remaining lime juice and Tabasco, and adjust seasonings.

Serves 6.

LOBSTER BISQUE

2 1-lb lobsters, cooked, with meat removed and diced, shells reserved
5 cups fish stock, page 194
2 stalks celery with leaves, finely chopped
1 large carrot, finely chopped
1 medium onion, chopped
2 cloves garlic, minced
3/4 cup butter
1 bay leaf
1/4 cup flour
1 cup heavy cream
Salt to taste
1 or 2 T sherry (optional)

Crush lobster claw and tail shells, tie securely in cheesecloth and add to the fish stock. Lightly saute celery, carrot, onion and garlic in 1/2 cup of the butter. Add to fish stock. Add the bay leaf and bring liquid to a boil, reduce heat and simmer until vegetables are tender, 10 to 15 minutes. Cool mixture slightly, remove shells and bay leaf, then puree mixture in a blender.

In a clean soup pot, melt remaining 1/4 cup butter; add flour and stir until smooth. Add pureed stock, stir well and simmer mixture for 10 minutes. Slowly add the heavy cream; add salt to taste. Add the diced lobster meat and sherry; heat thoroughly but don't let boil. Serve in warm bowls.

Serves 6-8.

CREAM OF SCALLOP SOUP

1 lb scallops, fresh or frozen, cut in half
4 cups fish stock, page 194
3 medium potatoes, peeled and quartered
2 medium onions, chopped
1 bay leaf
1 large sprig parsley
1/2 cup dry white wine
2 egg yolks
1 cup heavy cream
Salt and ground pepper to taste

Bring fish stock to a boil in a large pot. Add potatoes, onions, bay leaf and parsley. Simmer until potatoes are tender, about 20 minutes. Add scallops and wine and simmer another 5 or 6 minutes. Remove parsley and bay leaf; puree soup in blender, 2 cups at a time, until smooth (see Note). Pour pureed mixture into a clean pot and place over low heat.

In blender, add egg yolks and cream and blend until mixed. With blender operating, add 1 cup of the hot soup. Add cream mixture to soup in pot and stir well. Cook until thickened but not bubbling, and season to taste with salt and pepper.

Serves 6-8.

Note: If you wish, reserve some cooked scallops, chop them coarsely and add them for texture to the finished soup.

OYSTER STEW

1 pt fresh oysters with liquor
2 T butter
1 qt half and half cream, heated
Salt and pepper to taste
4 butter pats

Drain oysters (reserve liquor) and saute gently in melted butter until edges begin to curl. Heat oyster liquor to boiling, stir in cream and add oysters; do not let mixture boil. Add salt and pepper to taste. When ready to serve, pour into warm bowls and float a pat of butter on top of each serving.

Serves 4.

HEARTY BOUILLABAISSE

16 raw shrimp in shells
16 small hard-shell clams, well scrubbed
16 fresh mussels, scrubbed and threads removed
1 lb firm-fleshed fish (haddock, halibut or red snapper) cut into
    2-in. pieces
1 lb soft-fleshed fish (hake, sole or whiting), cut into 2-in. pieces
1 cup cooked lobster meat, cut up
1 cup fresh crabmeat
1/3 cup olive oil
2 cloves garlic, minced
2 large onions, chopped
2 leeks, washed and thinly sliced, white part only
4 fresh tomatoes, peeled and cubed
2 T minced fresh parsley
1/2 t dried thyme
1/4 t dried rosemary
1 bay leaf
1/8 t ground fennel seed
1/8 t saffron or tumeric
1 strip orange rind or lemon rind
Salt and freshly ground pepper to taste
6 cups hot fish stock, page 194
Hot water as needed
1/4 cup minced fresh parsley
French bread slices, sauteed in garlic oil until crisp and golden

Heat olive oil in a 10-quart pot; add garlic, onions and leeks; saute over low heat for 6 to 8 minutes, until soft. Add tomatoes and cook until soft, about 5 minutes. Add next 8 ingredients and stir, then add fish stock and simmer mixture about 10 minutes. Remove bay leaf; add shrimp, clams and mussels and simmer 5 to 6 minutes, until clams and mussels start to open. Add the firm-fleshed fish and soft-fleshed fish and simmer 5 minutes more, until fish is tender. Add more hot water if needed to cover ingredients. Add lobster and crabmeat last, heat thoroughly, adjust seasonings and sprinkle with 1/4 cup parsley. Place sauteed bread in the bottom of large heated soup bowls; place some of each kind of seafood over bread, then pour soup and vegetables over fish as desired.
    Serves 8-10.

CURRIED SHRIMP AND TOMATO BISQUE

1 lb raw shrimp, shelled and deveined
3 T butter
2 cloves garlic, minced
1 onion, chopped
2 t curry powder
1 bay leaf
2 large fresh tomatoes, peeled and cut into wedges
1 T tomato paste
3 cups fish stock, page 194
1/4 cup uncooked rice
Salt and ground pepper to taste
2 cups milk, heated
1 cup heavy cream

Melt butter in a large saucepan; add garlic and onion and saute until onion is limp. Add curry powder; stir and cook 2 more minutes. Add shrimp and cook over moderate heat until the outside turns pink and shrimp tests done when cut in half, about 5 minutes. Remove shrimp, cut in half if large, and set aside in a covered dish.

To the same pan add the next 4 ingredients and bring to a boil; add rice, salt and pepper and cook partly covered for 40 minutes. Add shrimp and heat through, then remove bay leaf, and cool slightly. Pour cooled mixture into blender, 3 cups at a time, and process until as smooth as desired. Add extra stock or water if mixture is too thick. Return pureed soup to a clean pot, stir in heated milk and heavy cream and cook until hot, but do not let boil. Adjust seasonings and serve hot or ice cold.

Serves 8-10.

OYSTER BISQUE

This is a strong-flavored bisque that is best aged for a day before serving.

1 pt oysters with liquor
1 t instant chicken broth
1 t grated onion
1 T minced fresh parsley
1 bay leaf
3 T butter
4 T flour
1 qt half and half cream, heated
1 cup heavy cream
Salt and pepper to taste
Dash Worcestershire sauce

Drain oysters, reserving liquor. Chop oysters well or put through coarse blade of meat grinder. Place oysters, oyster liquor, instant broth, onion, parsley and bay leaf in a saucepan and simmer gently for 2 to 3 minutes.

In a separate heavy pan, melt butter, add flour and cook until smooth. Remove from heat, add oyster mixture and mix well. Add creams and return to stove, heating gently until mixture thickens and bubbles just slightly. Remove bay leaf and add salt, pepper and Worcestershire sauce to taste.

Serves 6.

BILLI BI (Creamed Mussel Soup)

3 qts fresh mussels in shells, scrubbed and debearded
1 cup dry white wine or dry vermouth
1/4 cup chopped onion
1/4 cup chopped shallots
3 T minced fresh parsley
2 cups fish stock, page 194
1 cup heavy cream
2 egg yolks
Dash cayenne pepper
Salt to taste

In a large pot, combine mussels, wine, onion, shallots and parsley. Cover, bring to boil, then lower to simmer and cook about 5 minutes, or until mussels open. Remove pot from heat and strain liquid into a clean pot through a cheesecloth-lined strainer. Reserve mussels. Add fish stock to strained liquid and cook until hot; set aside.

In a blender container, add cream and egg yolks; blend a few seconds. With blender operating, slowly add 1 cup of the hot stock and blend until combined. Pour cream mixture into pot with stock, return to low heat and stir until mixture is thickened; do not let bubble or boil. Add cayenne and salt to taste. This very rich soup is delicious hot or cold.

Serves 4.

Note: The cooked mussel meats are usually saved for another dish, but if you have a food processor, you can puree some of the meats with 1 cup of the fish/mussel stock and add it to the soup. (You can also use a blender, but the mussels will not be processed as finely. If you wish, process them in the blender with some of the stock, then strain through a coarse strainer and add to the soup.)

POACHING LIQUIDS

Poaching liquids impart a variety of different flavors to the fish or shellfish cooked in them. The liquids can be strained and frozen, to be used again.

Any court bouillon can be used to cook shellfish, but keep the seasonings to a minimum if the seafood is to be served with a richly flavored sauce.

COURT BOUILLON

The difference between a court bouillon and a fish stock (page 194) is the addition of fish scraps to the fish stock.

8 cups water
1 cup dry white wine or dry vermouth
1 large onion, chopped
2 celery ribs with leaves, coarsely chopped
2 carrots, cut in thick slices
1 large leek, sliced, white part only
1/2 t dried tarragon
1 bay leaf
2 large sprigs parsley
6 whole peppercorns
1 or 2 t salt

Combine all ingredients and simmer for 1/2 hour. Strain broth into a clean pot. Bring to a boil, add whatever fish is to be poached and cook, timing from when the liquid begins to boil again. Reduce heat and simmer according to thickness of fish, allowing 10 minutes per inch of thickness at the thickest part for fresh fish, and 20 minutes per inch for frozen fish. Strain broth after poaching and freeze.
Makes 2 quarts.

SIMPLE POACHING BROTHS

For fish with very distinct flavors that you don't wish to hide, such as cod, halibut and haddock, combine equal parts of water and milk with a little salt, add the fish and poach according to directions. By reducing this liquid after cooking the fish, you can use it in place of fish stock in sauce recipes.

Salted water or fresh sea water is another simple poaching liquid for fish with distinct flavors such as sea bass and red snapper.

Reduced poaching liquids, except those with vinegar, can be used as the basis of an aspic to decorate chilled seafood, especially whole poached fish.

MAYONNAISE ASPIC

To be used as a coating on whole poached fish which is served chilled.

1 egg white
2 envelopes unflavored gelatin, softened in 1/2 cup cold water
2 cups plain or seasoned mayonnaise, pages 216 and 217
Poached seafood, well chilled
Thinly sliced vegetables for garnish
Mayonnaise-based sauce, pages 216 and 217

When the broth has been reduced to 4 cups, strain it and clarify as follows: bring broth to a boil, beat in egg white and beat constantly until frothy. Turn off heat and allow broth to settle for 10 minutes. Carefully strain again through a clean linen napkin (not too dense) which is lining a large strainer.

Add softened gelatin to clarified broth; bring to a boil and stir until gelatin is dissolved. Allow to cool. When mixture has almost jelled, stir 1 cup of it into 2 cups of mayonnaise. Coat poached, chilled seafood with mixture. If you wish to decorate the fish, add decoration to surface of mayonnaise gelatin. Chill. When the first coating of gelatin is firm, coat seafood with remaining plain gelatin. (Should the gelatin be too firm, heat it very slightly until it is spreadable.) Coat fish, chill and serve with a mayonnaise-based sauce. This makes a handsome presentation for any occasion.

Sauces & Marinades

Sauces enhance the taste as well as the presentation of fish and shellfish, no matter what cooking method is used. As a general rule, the milder, more delicately flavored fish and shellfish, such as sole, flounder, halibut, pike or scallops, do best with a rich but delicate sauce which does not overpower them. The more full-bodied, flavorful fish, such as bluefish, mackerel, tuna or eel, are well-complemented by tangy tomato, lemon juice or vinegar-based sauces. Herbed sauces are wonderful with any poached fish; cold fish and shellfish can take a simple mayonnaise sauce to a rich, tangy cocktail sauce. There is no limit to the imaginative ways in which sauces can be used.

Sauce terminology can sometimes be confusing. I will begin with the basic foundations, each with several variations.

Hot Sauces

VELOUTE
(Fish Stock Thickened with a Roux [Butter and Flour])

2 T butter
2 T flour
1 cup fish stock, page 194
Salt and pepper to taste

Melt butter in a saucepan and stir in flour. Cook over low heat until mixture is golden. Gradually stir in fish stock and continue stirring until sauce thickens. Simmer about 10 minutes and season to taste with salt and pepper.
Makes 1 cup sauce.

VELOUTE VARIATIONS

Rich Veloute Add 1 cup light cream blended with 2 or 3 egg yolks; gradually stir into basic sauce and heat until thickened. Do not let boil. **Makes 2 cups sauce.**

Seafood Sauces All the following amounts of cooked shellfish to the basic sauce: 1/2 cup finely chopped cooked shrimp, **or** 1/2 cup finely cut up cooked lobster meat, **or** 1/2 cup chopped cooked oysters (substitute 1/4 to 1/2 cup oyster liquor for fish stock in basic sauce), **or** 1/2 cup minced cooked clams (substitute 1/2 cup clam juice for fish stock in basic sauce), **or** 1/2 cup crabmeat.

Sauce Aurore Add 1/2 cup tomato paste to 1 cup basic veloute, then stir in 1/2 cup light cream blended with 2 egg yolks. Stir until thickened, but do not let boil. Season to taste. **Makes 2 cups.**

Sauce Mornay Add 1/4 cup grated Parmesan cheese to 1 cup basic sauce; stir until melted. Add 1/2 cup light cream blended with 2 egg yolks and cook until thickened. Add a dash of cayenne and salt if needed. **Makes 2 cups.**

Curry Veloute To 2 cups basic veloute, add 1/2 cup light cream and desired amount of curry powder; stir until hot. **Makes 2 cups.**

Sauce Soubise Add 1/2 cup finely chopped onion, sauteed but not browned, to 1 cup basic sauce. (Onion may be pureed first, then added.) **Makes about 1 1/2 cups.**

BECHAMEL (White Cream Sauce)

4 T butter
3 T flour
1/2 cup fish stock, page 194
1 cup milk or half and half cream
Salt and pepper to taste
Dash nutmeg (optional)

Melt butter and stir in flour; cook over low heat until golden. Add fish stock and stir until smooth; remove from heat and stir in milk or cream until well blended. Return to heat and cook, stirring constantly, until thickened. Continue cooking another 5 minutes; add seasonings to taste.
Makes about 1 1/2 cups.

BECHAMEL VARIATIONS

Tomato Sauce To basic sauce, add 1/4 cup tomato paste. **Makes 1 1/2 cups.**

Cheese Sauce To basic sauce, add 1 cup grated cheese (Swiss or cheddar), 1/2 t dry mustard and dash of cayenne pepper. Stir over low heat until cheese is melted. **Makes 2 cups.**

Egg Sauce To basic sauce, add 2 or 3 chopped hard-boiled eggs and 1 T minced parsley. **Makes 1 1/2 cups.**

White Wine Sauce To basic sauce, add 1/4-1/2 cup dry white wine blended with 2 egg yolks; heat but do not let boil, stirring constantly until thickened and smooth. **Makes about 2 cups.**

Mustard Sauce To basic sauce, add 1 t dry mustard and 1 T Dijon or other white wine mustard; stir well until blended and smooth. **Makes 1 1/2 cups.**

HOLLANDAISE SAUCE, BLENDER METHOD
(Rich Egg and Butter Sauce)

3 egg yolks
2 t water
2 T lemon juice
1/2 cup butter, melted
Salt to taste
Dash cayenne pepper

In blender container, combine egg yolks, water and lemon juice until smooth. With blender operating, slowly pour in melted butter. Pour contents of blender into saucepan and cook over low heat, stirring constantly, until sauce is thickened. Season to taste and serve warm. If sauce should separate, add a little boiling water and stir until smooth.
Makes 3/4 cup.
Note: This may not be the conventional way to make hollandaise, but it is quick and easy and works every time. If you prefer slightly thinner sauce, add more water, a little at a time.

HOLLANDAISE SAUCE VARIATIONS

Sauce Mousseline Gently blend together equal parts of Hollandaise and whipped cream. Makes a lovely, delicate sauce. Serve warm.

Sauce Bearnaise To 3 T wine vinegar in a saucepan, add 1 t dried tarragon, 2 t chopped green onion or shallots, dash salt and pepper; cook down until almost all liquid has evaporated. Add this mixture to the egg yolks and continue as for Hollandaise Sauce. Add more vinegar or lemon juice to taste. Serve warm. **Makes 3/4 cup.**

Tomato Bearnaise Stir 1 or 2 t tomato paste into Sauce Bearnaise and season to taste with salt and pepper. Serve warm. Makes 3/4 cup.

Sauce Verte Steam 1 cup washed fresh spinach leaves, 1/4 cup fresh watercress leaves, 1 T minced fresh parsley and 1 t dried tarragon for 5 minutes. Drain through a strainer, rinse in cold water and drain again. Press dry, and mash vegetables to a paste, removing any fibrous parts. Stir into 1 cup warm Hollandaise Sauce in a saucepan and place pan over hot water for a few minutes until flavors are blended. Serve warm. Makes about 1 1/2 cups.

Orange Hollandaise To 1 1/2 cups Hollandaise Sauce, add 2 T orange juice and 1 t grated orange rind. Serve warm. **Makes 1 1/2 cups.**

Creamy Garlic Hollandaise To basic Hollandaise Sauce, add 1 large clove garlic which has been pressed (use soft, pressed part only) and 1/4 cup whipped cream. Stir gently to blend flavors; serve warm. **Makes 1 cup.**

Chive Hollandaise To basic Hollandaise Sauce, add 1 1/2 t finely chopped chives. Serve warm. **Makes 3/4 cup.**

HOT SAUCES

FLUFFY LEMON SAUCE

Good on grilled steaks or fish cakes
2 T butter
2 T flour
1 1/4 cups milk
1/4 t paprika
1/2 cup mayonnaise
1 T lemon juice
Salt to taste

Melt butter and stir in flour, cooking until golden and bubbly. Add milk and cook over low heat until thickened, stirring constantly. Add paprika, mayonnaise and lemon juice; salt to taste.
Makes 1 3/4 cups.

SAUCE PROVENCALE

Good on broiled or baked fillets and steaks.

4 ripe tomatoes, peeled and cut into wedges
1/2 t sugar
2 T butter
1/4 cup chopped green onions
1/2 cup dry white wine or dry vermouth
1/2 cup butter
3 cloves garlic, minced
2 T chopped fresh parsley

Sprinkle tomatoes with sugar and set aside. Melt butter and cook green onion for 1 minute; add wine and cook until liquid is slightly reduced. Add remaining ingredients, including tomatoes, and heat for several minutes, until butter has melted and tomatoes are soft.
Makes about 2 1/2 cups.

TOMATO GRAVY

Good on fish cakes and croquettes.

1/4 cup each chopped onion and chopped green pepper
3 T butter
3 T flour
1/2 cup fish stock, page 194, or water
1 cup tomato puree
1 T sugar
1 t prepared horseradish
Salt and ground pepper to taste

Saute onion and green pepper in butter until onion is limp but not browned. Add flour and cook until bubbly; add fish stock and tomato puree, cook until thick and smooth. Add remaining ingredients and simmer 5 minutes to develop flavors.

Makes about 1 1/2 cups.

Hot Butters

Basic Clarified Butter Melt 1 pound butter over low heat. Remove from heat and let stand about 10 minutes. Skim any foam off the top, taking care not to disturb the solids on the bottom. The remaining clear yellow liquid can be removed and stored in the refrigerator for several weeks and used for cooking/sauteing, as it does not burn or splatter as does fresh butter. **Makes 2 cups.**

Beurre Noisette (Brown Butter) Melt the desired amount of butter in a small saucepan over medium heat. Cook until butter begins to turn pale brown, but does not burn. Remove from heat and stir in a little lemon juice. Serve hot. **Black Butter** is made by cooking the butter until it is darker, then adding chopped fresh parsley, capers and a little wine vinegar. Serve hot.

Lemon Butter To each 1/2 pound of butter, wisk in 3 T lemon juice and a little onion powder, paprika or whatever seasoning you wish. Serve hot. Overheating may cause separation, so watch carefully.

Garlic Butter To each 1/2 pound melted butter, add 1 or 2 cloves garlic, pressed, and simmer gently. Strain if you prefer and serve hot. For more flavor, add 1 T minced fresh parsley while simmering.

Beurre Verte (Green Butter) Into 1/2 pound soft butter, beat in the mashed spinach/watercress mixture used in Sauce Verte (page 211). You may sieve this mixture if you wish and then refrigerate, covered, until ready to use.

Minted Butter Melt 1/4 pound butter and add 2 T lemon juice, dash pepper and 2 T chopped, fresh mint. Serve hot.

Cold Butters

To 1/2 cup softened butter, add one of the following combinations:

2 t mashed, drained peppercorns; **or**

1/4 cup fresh basil and 2 T parsley (both finely minced), 1 T lemon juice, 2 T grated Parmesan cheese, dash pepper; **or**

2 minced shallots or green onions, cooked slowly in 1 T each white wine vinegar and lemon juice until liquid is almost evaporated; **or**

1 small, minced onion sauteed in 1 T melted butter until soft, 2 t paprika, 1/4 t black pepper; **or**

1 chopped lobster shell, cooked with 1/2 cup butter over hot water, strained through cheesecloth and refrigerated or frozen until needed. [Use as a flavoring for other sauces such as Lobster Veloute (page 209), or melt and serve over poached fish]; **or**

2 T minced shallots or green onions, 3 T minced parsley, 2 cloves pressed garlic, and 1 t lemon juice. (This is snail butter.)

These butters can be refrigerated and stored for several weeks, then used softened or melted over your favorite fish or shellfish. Flavored butters are especially good on broiled or grilled fish or shellfish, when they can be served slightly softened and allowed to melt over each portion.

———————◆•◆———————

Cold Sauces

BASIC MAYONNAISE

2 egg yolks, at room temperature
1/2 t salt, or more to taste
1/2 t dry mustard
Dash cayenne pepper
2 cups salad oil, or part salad and part olive oil, at room temperature
1 1/2 T white wine vinegar
1 T lemon juice

In a blender container or mixing bowl, beat together the first 4 ingredients until well mixed. Continue beating/blending and add oil, a few drops at a time, then in a slow, steady stream until all the oil is added and the mixture is thickened. Blend in the vinegar and lemon juice and adjust salt to taste. If the mixture should curdle (from adding the oil too fast), beat another egg yolk in a clean bowl and add the curdled mixture slowly, stirring constantly. This will restore the sauce to a smooth consistency.
Makes 2 cups.

BASIC MAYONNAISE VARIATIONS

Green Mayonnaise Add spinach-herb mixture (Sauce Verte, page 211) to 2 cups basic mayonnaise, blend well and chill. **Makes 2 cups.**

Louis Dressing (For crabmeat or shrimp salad) To 1 cup basic mayonnaise, add 1/4 cup chili sauce, 2 T minced fresh parsley, 2 T finely minced onion, and dash cayenne pepper. Mix well, then blend 6 T whipped heavy cream into mayonnaise mixture. **Makes about 1 1/4 cups.**

Tartar Sauce To 2 cups basic mayonnaise, add 3 T minced onion, 1 t lemon juice, 1/4 cup sweet pickle relish or chopped dill pickle, 1 t tarragon and 1 T minced parsley. Mix well and chill, allowing flavors to blend. **Makes 2 cups.**

Remoulade Sauce To 2 cups basic mayonnise, add 2 cloves minced garlic, 2 chopped hard-boiled eggs, 1 T minced parsley, 1 t dried tarragon, 2 t Dijon mustard, 1 T chopped capers and ground pepper to taste. **Makes 2 1/4 cups.**

Dill Mayonnaise To 1 cup basic mayonnaise, add 1/2 cup sour cream, 1 t dill weed, 1 t sugar, 1/2 t salt and dash ground pepper. **Makes 1 1/2 cups.**

Aioli Sauce (Garlic Mayonnaise) See page 197.

Curry Mayonnaise To 1 cup basic mayonnaise, add 1 t curry powder and 1 T chopped chutney. Blend well and chill to allow flavors to develop. **Makes 1 cup.**

◆ ● ◆

COCKTAIL SAUCE I

1 1/2 cups chili sauce
1 T tarragon vinegar
2 T prepared horseradish
1 t Worcestershire sauce
Dash Tabasco sauce
Ground pepper to taste

Combine all ingredients and chill well before serving. **Makes 1 1/2 cups.**

COCKTAIL SAUCE II

1/2 cup chili sauce or ketchup
1/2 t chili powder
1/8 t cayenne pepper
1 small clove garlic, pressed
2 t prepared horseradish
4 t lemon or lime juice

Combine all ingredients and chill. **Makes about 2/3 cup.**

Marinades

Marinades add extra flavor to all kinds of fish and shellfish and are especially good when broiling or grilling. Marinades keep seafood moist during cooking and act as tenderizers. Seasonings add interesting flavors.

The longer the fish is left in the marinade, the stronger the flavor will be, so take care that the fish doesn't lose its identity. The flavor of any fish can be enhanced by brushing the cut surfaces with lemon or lime juice about 1/2 hour before cooking.

◆ ◆ ◆

ALL-PURPOSE MARINADE

Good for swordfish, salmon and shark, or other firm-fleshed fish.

1/4 cup sweet or dry sherry
1/4 cup salad oil
2 T soy sauce
1 T brown sugar
1 or 2 cloves garlic, minced
Dash Worcestershire sauce
Ground pepper to taste

Combine all ingredients and marinate fish from 1 to 2 hours, depending on thickness. Use this sauce to baste while cooking.
Makes about 3/4 cup.

ROSEMARY-GARLIC MARINADE

Good for shrimp or fatty fish, such as swordfish, mackerel and bluefish.

1/2 cup salad oil
3 cloves garlic, minced
2 T lemon juice
2 T wine vinegar
1/2 t dried rosemary

Combine all ingredients and marinate seafood for 1 hour. Baste with sauce during cooking.
Makes 3/4 cup.

FRESH TOMATO SAUCE

Good for basting strongly flavored fish, such as bluefish, mackerel and tuna.

1 medium onion, chopped
1/2 cup chopped celery
3 T butter
2 cups fresh tomatoes, peeled, seeded and chopped
1/4 cup salad oil
1/4 cup distilled white vinegar
2 T lemon juice
1/3 cup brown sugar
2 T prepared mustard
1 T Worcestershire sauce
1 t salt
1 t ground pepper

Cook onion and celery in butter until onion is limp; add tomatoes and cook for about 5 minutes. Add remaining ingredients and simmer for 10 to 15 minutes, stirring often.
Makes 3 cups.

SOY AND GINGER MARINADE

Good for shrimp, sea bass steaks and swordfish steaks.

1/2 cup soy sauce
1/4 cup salad oil
3 T brown sugar or honey
1 clove garlic, minced
2 green onions, chopped
1 t grated fresh ginger root
1 T wine vinegar

Combine all ingredients and marinate fish or shellfish from 2 to 4 hours.
Makes about 1 cup.

ORANGE-SOY MARINADE

Good with light colored, firm-fleshed fish, such as swordfish, shark and halibut.

1/2 cup soy sauce
1/4 cup salad oil
1/4 cup ketchup
1/2 cup orange juice
2 t grated orange rind
2 T minced parsley
2 cloves garlic, minced
2 T lemon or lime juice
1/2 t ground pepper

Combine all ingredients and marinate fish for 1 hour. Use sauce for basting during cooking.
Makes about 1 1/2 cups.

GREEK MARINADE

Good for fish kebabs using firm-fleshed fish, shrimp or scallops.

1/2 cup dry white wine
1/4 cup olive or safflower oil
2 T lemon juice
1 T grated onion
1 clove garlic, minced
1 t dried oregano
1/2 t salt

Combine all ingredients and marinate fish or shellfish several hours so marinade can penetrate.
Makes about 1 cup.

Index

Appetizers

Atlantic croaker dip 35
Clams
  baked, oregano 150
  baked stuffed 151
  casino 149
  mushrooms stuffed with 150
  steamed 148
  steamed, David's herbed 148
Codfish croquettes 41
Crab, individual crepes 158
Haddock
  ceviche 50
  a la Security 48
Halibut with dips 56
Herring
  cold 62
  marinated 62
    with mustard sauce 64
    with sour cream 63
Mackerel, cold 68
Mussels
  broiled 169
  green 170
  steamed, herbed 170
Oysters
  baked, with variations 175
  raw on half-shell 173
Periwinkles, baked in
  garlic butter 178
Scallops, Polynesian 181
Shrimp
  canapes 191
  pickled 188
Tilefish
  quiches, individual 114
  spread 115
Whitefish, spread, smoked 142

Chowders; see also Soups and Stews

Bahamian fish 198
base, basic, with variations 195
fish stock 194

Cooking methods

baking 19
  hot-oven 19
broiling 19
frying, deep 21
grilling 23
pan frying 20
poaching 22
  broths, simple 206
  court bouillon 205
  liquids 205
sauteing 20

Entrees

Atlantic croaker 34
  saute 35
Bluefish 36
  baked in chips 39

in wine 37
orange-broiled 38
in sour cream 38
Catfish 128
  fried 129
  barbecued 129
Clams 146
  fried, in crumbs 151
  pasta with 149
  steamed 148
  steamed, David's herbed 148
Cod 40
  baked in herbs 41
  croquettes 41
  fishwich 42
  au gratin 42
Crab 152
  boiled 154
  curry 157
  and mushrooms with
    brown rice 155
Cusk 43
Eel 44
  baked in cream 47
  deep fried 45
  Provencale 45
  sauteed, in green sauce 46
Flounder, see Sole 94
Frogs' legs 130
  sauteed, basic 130
    with herbs 131
    with onions and
      mushrooms 131
    with tomatoes and garlic 131
Haddock 48
  cheese-baked 50
  finnan haddie casserole 52
  grilled, kabobs 49
  a la Security 48
  stuffed, Provencale 51
Hake 53
  fish cakes in tomato sauce 54
Halibut 55
  poached, with orange sauce 59
  steaks with mushroom
    stuffing 58
Herring 60
  baked 61
  baked with crumbs 61
Lobster 159
  boiled
    Maine 161
    tails, rock or spiny 163
  broiled
    tails, rock or spiny 163
  quiche a la Leonard 166
  stuffed, elegant 164
  tails in curry sauce, Danish 165
Mackerel 65
  baked, Espagnole 67
  broiled Bahamian 66
  grilled 66
Mussels 167
  Adriatic 169

fried	170
moules Susanne	171
steamed, herbed	170
Ocean perch	69
fried in paper	71
a l'Orange	70
Parmigiana	72
Oysters	172
Florentine	174
stuffing, for fish and poultry	176
Perch	132
broiled	134
poached walleye	133
yellow, in brown butter	133
Periwinkles	177
Pike	135
baked, with herbed cream sauce	137
Kiev	136
poached	136
Pollock	73
Red snapper	74
fillets amandine	75
heavenly	75
Salmon	76
broiled, herbed	77
mousse with cucumber and sour cream sauce	79
poached, with lemon sauce	78
stuffed with wild rice	80
Scallops	179
Coquilles Saint Jacques with crabmeat	183
fried, in almond coating	182
in honey and butter	182
sauteed with garlic and tomatoes	181
Sea bass	82
fried, with sweet and sour sauce	83
steamed, with sweet and sour sauce	83
Shad	85
baked, fillets	86
fillets amandine	86
roe	87
Shark	88
grilled, Oriental	89
oven-fried	89
teriyaki	90
Shrimp	184
boiled, spiced in beer	185
curry	186
fried, golden	189
oven-fried, with hot marmalade soy dip	190
pizzas, super	188
scampi	186
stir-fried, with asparagus	187
Smelt	91
deep fried	92
fry, Swedish, with anchovy-dill sauce	92

Sole	94
almond-fried	96
baked, with orange sauce	100
with curry, Danish	95
Ilena	97
nutty Parmesan	96
with onions and peppers, Chinese	98
Parmesan, with tomato sauce	99
Squid	101
baked stuffed I	103
baked stuffed II	104
fried	105
Striped bass	106
broiled, flambe	109
with crabmeat stuffing	108
in parchment	107
Swordfish	110
grilled	
marinated I	111
marinated II	111
sauteed with rosemary	112
Tilefish	113
with broiled spinach topping	114
quiches, individual	114
Trout	138
baked stuffed, in foil	140
campfire breakfast	139
grilled butterflied	140
poached, hot or cold	139
Tuna	116
grilled fresh	118
omelet, Gold Coast	119
Weakfish	123
sauteed, amandine	124
with tarragon	124
Whitefish	141
grilled	142
planked	143
Whiting	125
cracker-coated	126
marinated	126

Freezing information; see also General Information

freezing methods	15
storing frozen fish	14
thawing frozen fish	17

General Information 7

buying fish	10
how much to buy	14
freezing fish	15
market forms	12
nutritional value	18
packing fish for travel	17
storing fish	14
thawing fish	17

Marinades
all purpose   218
Greek   220
orange-soy   220
rosemary-garlic   218
soy and ginger   219
tomato, fresh   219

Preparation, basic
Flat fish
   how to dress   28
   how to fillet   30
   how to stuff   29
Round fish
   how to butterfly or split   31
   how to dress   24
   how to fillet   26
   how to steak   27
   how to stuff   25

Salads
Bluefish   37
Crab and fruit, Hawaiian   156
Crabmeat   155
Halibut ambrosia   56
Nicoise   118
Salmon, with pineapple   81
Salmon mousse with
   cucumber and sour cream
   sauce   79
Tilefish and fruit, chilled   115
Tuna, curried   122
Tuna with tomato aspic   120

Sandwiches
Scrod fishwich   42
Tuna rolls, hot   121

Sauces
Anchovy-dill, for smelt   92
Bechamel
   basic   209
   cheese   210
   egg   210
   mustard   210
   tomato   210
   wine   210
Butters
   cold, with variations   215
   hot
     black   214
     brown   214
     clarified   214
     garlic   214
     lemon   214
     minted   214
     Noisette   214
     verte   214
Cocktail
   I   217
   II   217
   hot (spicy)   173

Cucumber
   and sour cream, for salmon
     mousse   79
   dilled, for halibut   58
Hollandaise
   basic   210
   Bearnaise   211
     tomato   211
   chive   211
   garlic, creamy   211
   Mousseline   211
   orange   211
   verte   211
Lemon
   fluffy   212
   for salmon   78
Mayonnaise
   Aioli, for bouillabaise   197
   aspic   206
   basic   216
   curry   217
   dill   217
   dressing, Louis   216
   green   216
   Remoulade   217
   tartar   216
Mushroom, for salmon   80
Orange, for halibut   59
Orange, for sole   100
Provencale   212
Sour cream, cucumber and,
   for salmon mousse   79
Sweet and sour, for sea bass   84
Tomato
   gravy   213
   for hake   54
   for mackerel   67
   Provencale   212
   for sole   99
Veloute
   Aurore   209
   basic   208
   curry   209
   Mornay   209
   rich   209
   seafood   209
   Soubise   209

Soups and stews
Billi Bi   204
Bisque
   curried shrimp and tomato   202
   lobster   199
   oyster   203
Bouillabaise, hearty   201
Bourride with Aioli sauce   196
Scallop, cream of   200
Stew, oyster   200
Stock, fish   194